Every. Night. Of. The. Week. VEG

This book is for my kids:
James, Beau & Winter.

One day you will do, say or eat
something just like me and I hope when
you do the joy:cringe ratio is even.

I love you.

Every. Night. Of. The. Week.

VEG

Meat-free beyond Monday.
A zero-tolerance approach to bland.

Lucy Tweed

murdoch books

Sydney | London

Contents

Introduction 6
Dominating 8

1. Monday Cowboy Pasta Dreams
10

2. Toned-down Tuesdays
36

3. Saucy Wet Wednesdays
56

4. Carbs-filled-with-things Thursdays
84

5. Phat Snack Fridays

110

6. The Bold and the Beautiful Saturday Salads

136

7. Sunday Oeufs

162

8. Sweet Anytime Treats

190

Condiments 214
Thank You 219
Index 220

Introduction

**I need to start with a confession.
I'm not a vegetarian.**

Am I allowed to write a vegetarian book? Am I qualified?

A friend asked me if this book was going to be cheese heavy … I felt defensive. They didn't ask me that when I wrote a book with meat included.

I said 'No.'

I lied. Of course I use cheese. Sh*tloads.

Plus, a ton of eggs. And butter. Carbs – in all their glory. And – don't freak out – but this book includes VEGETABLES. LOADS.

What if we called it meat-free – that's probably more appropriate.

The object of this book is not to reduce fat, remove flavour or limit happiness. I'm not asking you to join a cult or commit to this every day.

It's about exploring variations. The possibilities. The fun.

It's about turning to the fridge crisper before the freezer.

My husband – a Kiwi raised on meat and veg – is known to respond to my food with 'This is so delicious! I can't believe there's no meat in it.'

And that's what makes this book essential.

Not what's lacking, but everything it has: flavour, texture and playfulness.

I love food. Most of it. I feel left out if I don't like something.

I went on a love crusade for mushrooms when I was young, and dear choko, I'm not there yet, but I admire you. Thank you, guac, for luring me into an avo-passion that hasn't ended. (I just don't think some foods are my people: natto, this is you, babe, sorry.)

Lifting veg from token to hero in a 'you-won't-notice-it's-meat-free' way is easy when you're pumped up about it. The upsell – or perhaps side-sell – comes naturally.

But there's a potential spanner in the (dinner) works: family. We must feed and nourish them while respecting their immature, undistinguished, sometimes revolting desires. Up to a point.

Growing up, my mum would take any opportunity to stuff a sun-warmed, slightly hairy baby bean picked straight from the vine into my gob. 'Taste this!' she'd exclaim.

My dad would normalise cuisines. 'This is San Chow Bow!', he'd announce proudly about yesterday's reheated bolognese with added peas and lettuce cups.

It's the excitement that matters most. And it's catching.

Getting food in mouths midweek is the destination, but the journey should be exploration, indulgence and laughter.

The chapters in this book are arranged as the days of the week.

Monday: quick-fix spaghetti bliss.

Tuesday: the day when we all lose a sock (HTF!?) –
it's best to put everything into one pan/pot or tray.

Wednesday: saucy wet Wednesday, of course.
All the stuff that needs spooning and mopping.

Thursday: carbs, stuffed with all the things.

Friday: stuffed/crumbed/fried snacks all round.
Make more, call the neighbours.

Saturday: big, beautiful and body proud salads.
These babies take the spotlight come BBQ day.

Sunday: all day oeuf. Breakfast, lunch and dinner eggs.

Extra play day: sweets. Quick-fix and bold adventures.
Did you even know vegetarians eat sweets!!!!?

Every recipe's deliciousness is subjective (not just
here, but EVERYWHERE!), and I urge you to tweak them
to suit yourself and your family.

If in doubt, just crumb it and add tomato sauce.
Most kids will eat a small section of cow dung
if served that way*. And I still add token veg to
everything because it confuses them, and I like
mind games like that.

Always play with your food,

Lucy x

*not tested yet

Dominating

TIPS & TRICKS OF THE TRADE

Being the alpha in the kitchen is crucial. These are
the things I do to make the most of ingredients.

Leafy guys

- Straight up think about the journey produce
  has been on to get to your fridge. We all need
  a soak and a big drink after a long trip and veg
  is no different.

- Storing your herbs properly can mean the
  difference between 3 and 8 days of freshness.
  Rinse and wrap them in paper towel, put them
  in a snap-lock bag or airtight container and
  toss them back in the fridge.

- Trimming and washing lettuce before you pack
  it away is both a time-saver and an extender.

- Icing salad herbs is a stylist trick to keep things
  perky on set, and worth doing at home too. At the
  start of making a big salad, pick all your herbs
  and put them in a large bowl of icy water for
  about 20 minutes. They will drink and spring up.

Cold queen

- When herbs do start to lose their vibrancy, pick the
  leaves and discard any that have decayed. Blend
  the rest with olive oil and store in a jar in the fridge,
  or freeze in ice-cube trays. What you have now is
  the perfect flavour hit for pastas and soups, or to
  stir through mayo for a great sambo condiment.

- Make enough salad dressing for a week, store it
  in a jar and splash it liberally when needed.

- Don't discard pickle juice and olive brine!!! Just top
  them up with veg offcuts, or add them to a martini.

- For ultra-crisp carrots, celery and radish, store
  them in a container in the fridge with a puddle
  of water.

Freezer hacks

- When ordering takeaway, buy a second container of steamed rice for the freezer. That's half a meal done on time-poor nights.

- Save your stale bread. Trim off the dry crusts, tear the bread into chunks and freeze it. When you need a crispy crouton, just toss with oil and salt and bake until golden.

- Make double of anything that you can freeze. Ragu, soup, gnocchi, dumplings.

- Don't be a freezer elitist. Having back-up frozen veg can change a last-minute dinner from boring and beige to a jazzy little festival of food.

Longer leftovers

- If you've made more filling for wontons or dumplings than you can deal with, any excess makes a great midweek stir-fry – it's already seasoned and full of great things.

- A stale loaf of bread can be revived by wetting it thoroughly under cool running water, then placing it into a preheated oven at 200°C (400°F) for 15 minutes, or until crispy, fresh and bouncy. It's like magic.

- You can also use up stale bread by breaking it into chunks then blending it in a food processor to form fine crumbs – perfect to use later in pangrattato, as a lasagne topping, or for general breadcrumbing.

- Blend left-over roast vegetables with tinned tomatoes for the ultimate pizza sauce or with stock and cream for a velvety soup.

Pantry party

- Use round sticky dots or a black marker to label the top of your spice jars. I store mine in a big Tupperware container and this saves me from the intensely irritating lift-and-search method.

- Storing dry goods in jars keeps them fresh, plus it means basics like flour, sugar and rice all get topped up before they run out because you can see them.

- Cool, dark and dry – the pantry is the favoured place for onions, garlic and spuds. Remove any packaging and pop them in a cloth bag or basket.

- Extreme trigger warning: throughout this book I regularly call for chicken- and beef-style stock. These readily available veg-based stocks are so good (in flavour and ingredients), I used them for years BEFORE I realised they were vegetarian.

There is nothing as truly weeknight as a pot of pasta.

Eight minutes to al dente felt like an hour when I was a kid. Hungry from mucking about with ponies, pretending to be a cowboy and running up and down hills, a bowl of long or short was the ultimate inside hug of comfort before bed. It still is, though the ponies are now my kids, and the hills are laundry piles in the hallway.

I like pasta in every size, shape and colour – salty, chewy, crispy, saucy, soft, slippery.

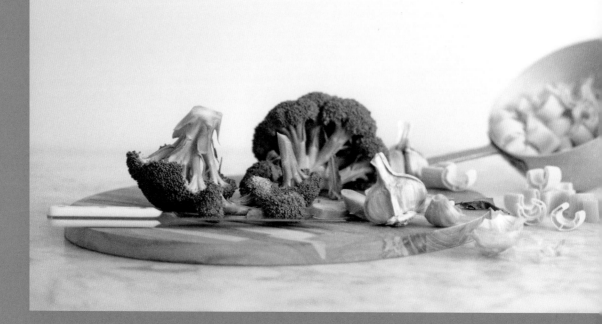

Monday Cowboy Pasta Dreams

One-Pot Business

Internal dialogue
appreciation post.

1 tablespoon dijon mustard
¼ cup (60 ml) lemon juice
2 tablespoons extra virgin olive oil
1 brown onion, thinly sliced
½ cup (110 g) marinated
    artichokes, chopped
½ cup (110 g) pitted green olives
1 tablespoon capers
2 garlic cloves, sliced
¼ cup (60 ml) white wine
¼ cup (60 g) salted butter
250 g (9 oz) rigatoni
10 basil leaves

10 dill sprigs
3 cups (750 ml) vegetable stock
¼ cup (25 g) finely
    grated parmesan
2 tablespoons finely grated
    lemon zest

OPTIONAL INGREDIENTS
chicken

I can't help it; I think about roast chicken when I think about this dish – I don't know why!

Can you be vegetarian and still think about meat, or is that a complete faux pas? Not being one myself, I don't know all the finer points ... all I know is this is a very delicious dish. And if your thoughts are going to offend, you should probably keep them to yourself.

Although that could be boring.

Due to the size of the pasta I've used here, this only serves 2. You could certainly double everything to serve 4, but choose a smaller pasta like ditalini, or use a bigger pot (keep stirring though so everyone gets a go being on the bottom with all the saucy juice).

Combine the dijon and lemon juice. Set aside.

Heat the olive oil in a large deep frying pan over medium–high heat. Pan-fry the onion for 5 minutes, until soft, then add the artichokes, olives and capers and cook until the edges have a golden brown crust, around 5 minutes. Add the garlic and sauté for 2 minutes.

Pour in the wine and boil, stirring, to deglaze the pan, or until the wine has mostly evaporated. Add the butter and stir well.

Add the rigatoni and herbs. Pour the mustard/lemon juice mix and the stock on top of the pasta.

Cover with a lid and simmer on the stove for 25 minutes, until cooked and beginning to crisp on the edge. The pasta should be al dente and still bubbling.

Stir through the parmesan and lemon zest before serving.

Serves 2

Supergreens Gnudi

Crispy, soft, plump, chunky, rough dumplings – I think we can all relate. Send (G)nudis stat.

500 g (1 lb 2 oz) frozen spinach, kale or any other leafy green
500 g (1 lb 2 oz) fresh ricotta (the deli kind in a basket because it's drier)
4 eggs, lightly whisked
1 cup (100 g) finely grated parmesan
pinch of ground nutmeg
1 cup (150 g) plain (all-purpose) flour
semolina, for sprinkling
¼ cup (50 g) buckwheat

veg oil, for frying
1½ tablespoons extra virgin olive oil
2 tablespoons salted butter
1 garlic clove, finely chopped
1 teaspoon chilli flakes
30 g (1 oz) rocket (arugula)
2 tablespoons lemon juice
100 g (3½ oz) halloumi, grated
2 tablespoons finely grated lemon zest

OPTIONAL INGREDIENTS
plates

If you are undone by the sin* of conveniently prepared frozen spinach, then you could always de-spine, cook, squeeze and chop fresh if you like. You'll need approximately 75 kg (165 lb) of fresh leaves to yield 2 cups once wilted (estimating the weight of cooked-down leafy greens from a fresh bunch is pointless).

Thaw, squeeze and chop the greens in a food processor or with a knife. The blitzing level is up to you. The leafier bits are harder to roll, but rude, nude and rustic is what's so great about these gnudi, so I blitz for a bit, remove half and purée the rest.

Reunite the spinach in a bowl and add in the ricotta, eggs, parmesan, nutmeg and flour. Mix well to combine.

You can add herbs, garlic or zest to the dumplings but I like to boss my dinner about not the other way around. Keep it simple and you can whip this out of the freezer anytime. Pick your flavours then.

Prep a tray or plastic container with baking paper so you can layer these. Have a small bowl of semolina for sprinkling at the ready.

Using two tablespoons, one to scoop and one to scrape, shape the dough into little dumplings and dollop them onto the tray.** Sprinkle a bit of semolina over them as you go to prevent them sticking to each other.***

Fry the buckwheat in 1 cm (½ inch) veg oil in a small saucepan over high heat. They will get crispy and some will puff like mini popcorn in less than 10 seconds. Scoop these buckinis out onto paper towel and set aside.

You can cook (fresh or frozen) gnudi just as you would gnocchi, in plenty of simmering salted water, scooping them out as they float and tossing with your fave sauce, but my preference is to cook them like potstickers. Choose a non-stick frying pan that can hold as many serves as you'd like to make in a single layer – usually about 20 would be the most! Heat 1½ tablespoons olive oil over medium heat and place the gnudi in a single layer with a bit of space between each one.

As they begin to sizzle, add some water so that it comes halfway up the side of the dumplings. Cover the pan with a lid and allow it to simmer for 5–8 minutes. Listen for a change in fry sound from watery bubble to oily sizzle. Gently toss and loosen the gnudi and push to the side. Add the butter and, when it foams, add the garlic, chilli and rocket. Toss the whole lot for a few minutes, until the garlic softens slightly, then add in the lemon juice for a final stir through.

Cover in halloumi, lemon zest and buckinis before serving.

---

* Not at all a sin: frozen spinach is highly nutritious and delicious!

** If you have neither skill nor patience for quenelling, then you could pipe the dumplings onto the tray using a snap-lock bag with the corner snipped off.

*** To freeze gnudi, arrange the freezer so you can slide the entire tray in, then after 4 hours you can move them into a snap-lock bag.

Serves 4–6

¾ cup (185 g) softened
  salted butter
¼ cup (40 g) Vegemite*
500 g (1 lb 2 oz) bucatini
2 garlic cloves, finely chopped
2 tablespoons freshly ground
  black pepper
2 tablespoons extra virgin olive oil
1½ cups (150 g) grated pecorino
1½ cups (150 g) grated
  grana padano

Cacio (in my mind) is not an ingredient ... it's a situation. Catchy, sticky cheese will coat the pan, forks, tongs, spoons, bowls – it's a f*cking nightmare.

My hack: just soak everything overnight in cold water then, when that doesn't work, simply throw all the dishes out (plus everything you've attempted to clean them with). Nonetheless, this pasta is worth every drop of elbow grease.

In a standmixer fitted with the paddle attachment, mix the butter and Vegemite until well combined.**

Cook the pasta in a large saucepan of heavily salted water with a timer set to 2 minutes before al dente (as the packet directs).

Meanwhile, in a large heavy-based non-stick frying pan, fry the garlic and pepper in olive oil over medium heat until fragrant, about 4 minutes.

Add about ¼ cup (60 g) of the Vegemite butter and swirl it around in the resulting insane froth until the smell makes your mouth water.

Add 1 cup (250 ml) of pasta water to the pan and simmer for 1 minute.

Tong the pasta straight over from the cloudy boiling water into the buttery pan.

Reduce the heat to low and add the grated cheeses in ½ cup (50 g) increments, tossing it around with tongs. This is not a big tall toss, more a shimmy, shake, fold and stir.

Add another scoop of pasta water if you like – the stirring-water-butter-cheese-pasta-gluten makes the sauce in this one. It's the riz-oh-toe effect, yeah?

Remove the pan from the heat and make sure it's all as glossy, slippery and silky as something worn to the Met Gala. Add more water if you need to.

Serve immediately. This one benefits from that artful tonged swirl we all aspire to – but that's just for presentation. If you enjoy this dish as much as I do, it doesn't matter how it flops from the pan to the bowl to the mouth, as long as it doesn't hit your chin while hot.

* If Vegemite is unavailable or you are ultimately opposed to this ingredient, sub it out for Marmite or even miso for that umami punch.

** Srsly, make a second batch and continue beating until the butter is creamed. Chuck it in a jar for camping or at-home toast – now you can have 'people' make you toast without the ratio being f*cked up.

Serves 4

Vegemite Cacio e Pepe

Start by calling shotty on NOT cleaning up after this dinner.

Zucchini Carbonara

To cream or not to cream –
actually it's not a question.

1 leek, white part only, julienned
2 tablespoons extra virgin olive oil
1 garlic clove, coarsely chopped
¼ cup (60 g) salted butter
2 large zucchini (courgettes),
   julienned
10 basil leaves, large ones sliced,
   small kept whole
1 egg
2 egg yolks
2 cups (200 g) finely
   grated parmesan

500 g (1 lb 2 oz) spaghetti
fine salt and freshly ground
   black pepper, to taste

The creamy texture of this dish is created with egg yolk, cheese, pasta water and a very attentive level of stirring, swirling and tossing at the right time.

You cannot walk away from this dish. It's like an attention-demanding 4-year-old attempting something completely unspectacular ... if you avert your eyes for even a second then the result will be a claggy, unemulsified mess. And as most of us with kids will attest, if your child is unemulsified, well, you just have to start again.

In a large frying pan over medium heat, sauté the leek for 3 minutes in olive oil, until it begins to darken and crisp up.

Add the garlic and butter and cook for a further 2 minutes.

Finally add the zucchini and basil and toss through for 1 minute. This step is to soften the zucchini, not necessarily cook it.

Remove the pan from the heat.

Meanwhile, combine the egg, yolks and grated cheese in a large serving bowl. Mix well.

Cook the pasta in a large saucepan of heavily salted water to al dente.

Ladle a few tablespoons of pasta water into the egg and parmesan mixture to temper it, then top with the sautéed veg.

Tong the steaming hot pasta straight over from the cloudy boiling water to the serving bowl.* Toss it through the mixture quickly for at least 1 minute to combine it all. Season as needed.

The eggs will begin to set into a creamy texture, and the parmesan will melt and become a deliciously perfect host to tendrils of spaghetti, zucchini and leek.

---

* If you'd rather drain than tong your spaghetti into the bowl, then make sure to reserve 1 cup (250 ml) of pasta water before doing so. This is possibly the most important ingredient in any pasta dish, and slowly we are understanding the concept, but it still has to be stressed every time.

Serves 4

Sweet Corn Pillows

Sometimes the fancy just happens and you find yourself dining.

¼ cup (50 g) corn kernels,
 drained if from a tin
125 g (4½ oz) tinned
 creamed corn
235 g (8½ oz) fresh ricotta
1 teaspoon finely grated lime zest
¼ teaspoon paprika
¼ teaspoon garlic powder
¼ teaspoon white pepper
1 tablespoon finely snipped chives
1 egg white, whisked until foamy
 (not stiff)
40 round gow gee wrappers

DESIRABLE SAUCE
2½ tablespoons white miso paste
½ cup (125 ml) white wine
⅔ cup (160 g) cold salted butter,
 cubed
1 long red chilli, seeds removed,
 finely diced

OPTIONAL INGREDIENTS
lots of parmy and linen napkins

Often when flavours meet, the exchange exemplifies a perfect mutualism: Corn + Miso = 2gether 4eva (with butter as a lubricant).

Combine both the corns, the ricotta, lime zest, paprika, garlic powder, pepper and chives in a bowl and mix well. Fold the egg white through gently.

Lightly flour a large tray where you can rest your dumplings as you make them.

Using a brush and water, lightly wet one side of a gow gee wrapper. Place a tablespoon of corn mixture in the centre of each wrapper, leaving a 1 cm (½ inch) edge. Place another wrapper over the top and seal all around with your fingers, pushing out as many air pockets as possible – you want the dumpling/ravioli/pillows to remain full once cooked and not deflated and saggy ... don't get distracted.* Set the pillows aside on the floured tray until ready to cook.**

For the desirable sauce, whisk together the miso paste and white wine in a large frying pan over medium heat until combined and beginning to bubble, around 2 minutes. Add in the cold butter and continue to whisk so that it emulsifies as it melts. Sprinkle with the chilli. Set aside and keep warm.

When you are ready, poach the pillows in plenty of salted simmering water for 5 minutes. Scoop the pillows out with a slotted spoon, place them directly into the pan of desirable sauce and gently swish around. Add a scoop of pasta water if the sauce needs loosening.

This last saucy bit is best done in batches of two serves, but you can be bold and ignore me and I am sure it will be absolutely fine.

* Oh! Insert a fancy step here! If this is a 'dinner party/extra moment' then you should absolutely make the filling mound neat and tidy by pressing a shot glass over the top, then use a 10 cm (4 inch) cookie cutter to trim the edges to perfection à la 90s perfect food intention.

** These dumplings are ideal frozen and whipped out straight into boiling water. You can freeze them for a few months in an airtight container.

Serves 6–8 (5–6 pillows each)

parmesan, for sprinkling

NOODLE DOUGH
2 cups (300 g) tipo 00 flour
1 teaspoon fine salt
⅔ cup (170 ml) warm water
3 tablespoons extra virgin olive oil
semolina, for dusting

SAUCE
650 g (1 lb 7 oz) tomatoes,
    coarsely chopped
1 leek, white and pale green parts
    only, sliced into 1 cm (½ inch)
    thick rounds
3 tablespoons fresh
    oregano leaves
1 teaspoon sea salt flakes,
    plus extra for sprinkling
1 teaspoon freshly ground
    black pepper
2 tablespoons extra virgin olive oil
½ cup (125 ml) vodka
⅓ cup (80 ml) thick (double)
    cream

OPTIONAL INGREDIENTS
martinis, of course

It's far-fetched to include a homemade pasta dough recipe for a Monday night, but a) you'll rejoice at knowing this super slack and utterly satisfying shape-making technique, and b) you can just sub it out for some perky little favourite shape on Monday, and have this beauty up your sleeve for showing off on the weekend with friends and/or enemies.

For the noodle dough, place the flour and salt in the bowl of a standmixer fitted with the dough hook and set the speed to low. Add the water and oil in a slow, steady stream, mixing until a ball forms, around 1–2 minutes. Increase to medium speed and mix for 4–5 minutes, or until the dough is soft and elastic. Wrap in plastic wrap and rest for 20 minutes (pasta is lucky with the amount of enforced resting it goes through!).

This is the fun/precarious bit. Holding the rested ball over a semolina-dusted surface, begin snipping small slivers off the ball with scissors. You will gain momentum. Just remember to adjust your fingers away from the snipping zone as you do. Little eye shapes will fall to the bench and they will have an organic rib or curl along their edge, which makes for the perfect sauce boat.

If you realise your snipping has been somewhat irregular, just snip the larger ones in half. There's no rule to how big they should be – you can make them tiny if you like! I have made 1.5 cm (⅝ inch) ones for this recipe. Cover them with a cloth until ready to use or freeze them for anticipated post-club dining.

Preheat the oven to 200°C (400°F) fan-forced.

For the sauce, massage the tomatoes, leek, oregano, salt and pepper with the oil in a bowl. Spread out in a flameproof baking dish and roast for 25 minutes.

Transfer the tomato mixture to a large jug or bowl and blend with a stick blender until it becomes a smooth purée. Push this mix through a sieve so it's extra fine. (I understand this is excessive. This step is possibly more for those who discotheque. You can, of course, opt for the tracksuit version and not sieve at all.)

You should have about 2 cups (500 ml) of sauce, which is about what you would get in a bottle of bought passata (this is an ultimate shortcut hint for you!).

Place the baking dish over high heat, pour in the vodka and boil, stirring to deglaze (but not for too long – this is one time you don't want the booze burning completely off). Add the tomato purée and bring it to a simmer. Stir through the cream and remove the dish from the heat.

Bring a big pot of salted water to a rapid boil and add the pasta. Once the pasta floats to the surface (about 2 minutes), use a slotted spoon to scoop the pasta from the boiling water and place straight into the vodka sauce.

Add a scoop of pasta water and toss well before covering in an 80s discotheque level of snowy parmesan.

Serves 4

Snipped Noodles in Vodka Sauce

Pasta and dancing? No one
knew about gluten then.

Ribbons in Crackling Oil

Content warning: birth
stories and boiling oil.

250 g (9 oz) fresh lasagne sheets
2 teaspoons szechuan
    peppercorns
2 teaspoons chilli flakes
2 tablespoons finely grated
    fresh ginger
4 garlic cloves, finely chopped
1 teaspoon Chinese five-spice
1 tablespoon sesame seeds
1 tablespoon dark soy sauce
1 tablespoon soy sauce
1 teaspoon black vinegar
½ teaspoon fine salt

2 teaspoons sesame oil
2 spring onions (scallions),
    white parts minced, green tops
    thinly sliced and set aside
1 cup (250 ml) peanut oil
1 bunch Chinese water spinach,*
    cut into 5 cm (2 inch) lengths

OPTIONAL INGREDIENTS
shaved celery and celery tops

When my last baby was slow to arrive, I tried a bunch of stuff to move things along. Jumping on a trampoline and eating crackling oil noodles were my favourite, but both seemed to comfort her as much as me. Also like me, when she's ready to roll, she has very little patience. Thankfully we made it to the hospital with about 8 minutes to spare.

Crackling oil is also called 'boiling oil' (it just feels a little terrifying put like that as we don't want to actually boil it). You want your oil hot enough so that when it's poured on herbs, spices, etc., it immediately starts to crackle, bubble and froth.

Cut the fresh lasagne sheets into ribbons – the thickness is up to you, I'm into super-fat 3 cm (1¼ inch) ribbons. It's fun. But 1–1.5 cm (½–⅝ inch) thick is great. (Instead of sheets, you can use really fat pappardelle, or the frilly-edged noodles you can sometimes find in Asian supermarkets.)

Roughly grind the szechuan peppercorns and chilli flakes in a mortar and pestle and transfer to a heatproof serving bowl. Add the ginger, garlic, Chinese five-spice, sesame seeds, dark soy sauce, soy sauce, black vinegar, salt, sesame oil and the white part of the spring onions.

Heat the peanut oil in a large heavy-based saucepan over medium heat until it reaches shimmering point (it can begin to smoke but not excessively).

Meanwhile, bring lots of salted water to the boil in a large pot. Cook the lasagne ribbons according to packet directions until 1 minute before al dente, then add the Chinese water spinach and spring onion tops and cook for 1 minute more.

Carefully remove the shimmering oil from the heat and immediately pour it over the aromatics in the bowl. Add the well-drained pasta and stir everything together well.

Serve immediately.

* Chinese water spinach is a favourite but very seasonal green where I live. Swap out for bok choy or Chinese broccoli (gai lan) – regular broccoli is great too!

Serves 4

Cheese & Tomato Lasagne

This is an incredibly successful lasagne. Like, corporate-box successful.

BIG BATCH BESHY
4 quantities Baby Beshy (page 215)
¾ cup (105 g) grated
  mozzarella
½–1 cup (50–100 g) grated
  cheddar

SAUCE
5–6 tomatoes, coarsely chopped
6 garlic cloves, smashed
¼ cup (7 g) oregano leaves,
  tightly packed, chopped
2 tablespoons red wine vinegar

1 teaspoon white
  (granulated) sugar
1 teaspoon fine salt,
  plus a pinch extra
1 tablespoon extra virgin olive oil,
  plus extra for drizzling
700 g (1 lb 9 oz) tomato passata
  (puréed tomatoes)
3 stalks basil
freshly ground black pepper,
  to taste

250 g (9 oz) fresh lasagne sheets,
  which I will be blanching,
  regardless of pack instructions
110 g (3¾ oz) buffalo mozzarella
  ball, sliced into 6–7 rounds
  (as many as you can manage,
  actually)
½ cup (30 g) panko breadcrumbs*
¼ cup (25 g) finely grated
  parmesan

OPTIONAL INGREDIENTS
green salad at the ready

Tangy, cheesy, carby, saucy = vibe. The combination of tomatoes, fresh and tangy and thick and sweet, is what makes this dish exciting.

Make a big batch of beshy and add the cheeses, stirring over medium heat until you have a smooth sauce, around 5 minutes.

I mean, you could stop there. Just fondue your evening away, naked.

Although, that kind of carry-on should at least be reserved for Thursday.

In a mixing bowl, toss the tomatoes with two-thirds of the smashed garlic, half the oregano, the red wine vinegar, sugar and salt (think SUPER tangy). Set this aside to macerate for 10 minutes or so.

In a medium saucepan over medium heat, sauté the remaining garlic with a pinch of salt and 1 tablespoon of olive oil for

2 minutes, until golden. Add the passata, the remaining oregano and the whole basil stalks and season with freshly ground black pepper. Simmer for 10 minutes, until it becomes lava-like and rich. Set aside to cool.

Meanwhile, blanch the lasagne sheets and set aside in cool water to stop them sticking.

Remove the basil stalks from the sauce, then pour the sauce over the macerating tomatoes and toss well.

Preheat the oven to 200°C (400°F) fan-forced.

Take a 30 x 7 cm (12 x 2¾ inch) round ovenproof dish and slap 2 tablespoons of tomato sauce and a drizzle of olive oil on the bottom. Then layer: pasta, toms, beshy, pasta, toms, beshy, pasta etc. – finish with pasta and beshy. Top with fat slices of buffalo mozzarella, a sprinkling of panko crumbs and grated parmy.

Bake for 30 minutes, then remove it from the oven and let it sit for a while before eating so you don't liquefy from the inside out as a result of the searing tomato and cheese heat.

Please try this. It is so, so delicious.

---

* I use KookAKrumb panko to avoid palm oil!

Serves 6–8

800 g (1 lb 12 oz) kent pumpkin (squash), peeled and cut into 4 cm (1½ inch) chunks
4 tablespoons extra virgin olive oil, plus extra for drizzling
1 egg yolk
½ cup (50 g) finely grated parmesan
pinch of ground nutmeg
fine salt and freshly ground black pepper, to season
1½ cups (220 g) plain (all-purpose) flour

260 g (9¼ oz) tomato passata (puréed tomatoes)
2 tablespoons single (pure) cream
2 tablespoons white wine
40 sage leaves
150 g (5½ oz) soft blue cheese, coarsely chopped
150 g (5½ oz) mozzarella, coarsely chopped

SALAD
2 teaspoons honey
2 tablespoons red wine vinegar
2 small pears, thinly sliced
3 tablespoons extra virgin olive oil
120 g (4¼ oz) rocket (arugula)
sea salt flakes and freshly ground black pepper, to taste

OPTIONAL INGREDIENTS
parmy on the salad

It was during the creation of this particular dish that I pondered my cheese-consumption levels.

While this book is vegetarian and relies on a bounty of beautiful vegetables, I can't and happily don't claim that it's light on anything really – flavour especially.

As it turns out, the cheese ratio is very well balanced with all the lemon, garlic and fresh things.

Of course you could omit the cheese, but then that is, perhaps, another story ...

Preheat the oven to 200°C (400°F) fan-forced.

Toss the chopped pumpkin with 2 tablespoons olive oil and place on a baking tray lined with baking paper. Bake for 40 minutes, until lightly browned on the edges and soft.

Mash the cooled pumpkin in a large mixing bowl. Add the egg yolk, parmy and nutmeg and stir with a fork until just combined. Season, then add 1 cup (150 g) of flour, gradually adding more and stirring until the dough is just not sticky. Don't over-stir: you don't want to activate the flour. The dough should remain soft.

Turn the dough out onto a lightly floured surface and knead gently.

Divide the dough into 6–8 balls, then roll each one into a 1.5 cm (⅝ inch) thick log. Cut each log into 1 cm (½ inch) sections so you have little puffy pillow rectangles.*

Grease a tray with 1 tablespoon of the olive oil and place it next to your stovetop, ready to catch the gnocchi. Bring a large saucepan of salted water to a rapid simmer. Poach about 20 gnocchi at a time. Remove the gnocchi with a slotted spoon when they float to the top – around 1 minute – and place on the oiled tray.

In the base of a large baking dish, place 1 tablespoon olive oil, the passata, cream, white wine and half the sage leaves and mix together. Nestle the gnocchi in, then top with the remaining sage and cheeses.

Drizzle with olive oil and place in the oven until golden and bubbling, about 20 minutes.

Meanwhile, in a salad bowl, combine the honey and red wine vinegar and toss the pear in the mixture until it's coated. Just before serving, add the olive oil, rocket and parmesan. Season with S+P and toss well.

---

* If you make more than you need, freeze the leftovers for another time. They'll keep for a few months in an airtight container. Throw frozen gnocchi straight into boiling water and cook as above.

Serves 4

Baked Pumpkin Gnocchi

My 'double down' on cheese
instinct is pretty intense.

Vegan Pad Thai

Actually the vegan is optional, as are the eggs in this recipe.

500 g (1 lb 2 oz) firm tofu, crumbled

3 eggs, lightly whisked (optional – obviously must be removed for vegans)

175 g (6 oz) oyster mushrooms, sliced

1 bunch garlic chives, cut into 5 cm (2 inch) strips (or 1 red/brown onion, finely sliced)

1 baby wombok or ½ big wombok, shredded

200 g (7 oz) rice noodles, soaked in cold water for 1 hour

1 cup (115 g) bean sprouts, hairy ends picked off

1 cup (30 g) coriander (cilantro) leaves

⅓ cup (50 g) chopped toasted peanuts

1 lime, cut into wedges

PAD THAI SAUCE

2 tablespoons tamarind paste

2 tablespoons white miso paste

2 tablespoons soy sauce

4 tablespoons soft brown sugar

1 tablespoon sesame oil

PAD THAI PASTE

½ cup (125 ml) peanut oil

1 tablespoon fine salt

1 lemongrass stem, the first 10–15 cm (4–6 inches) only, roughly chopped

1 makrut lime leaf, chopped

1 spring onion (scallion), white and green parts, chopped

1 cm (½ inch) knob of ginger, peeled and chopped

1 garlic clove, chopped

OPTIONAL INGREDIENTS

eggs – just get a marker and cross them out if they are that offensive

Don't freak. But it's vegan without cheese. Like, for reals vegan. Until I add the optional eggs. Please adapt by ignoring them.

Also, if you haven't crumbled tofu yet you MUST try it – it's soft, bouncy and basically a vessel for whatever flavour you want!

In a small bowl, stir the tamarind, miso, soy, brown sugar and sesame oil until smooth. This will be the pad Thai sauce.

Then, using a food processor or stick blender, blend the peanut oil (reserving 2 tablespoons for greasing the pan when frying batches of veg), salt, lemongrass, lime leaf, spring onion, ginger and garlic to make the pad Thai paste.

Crumble and fry the tofu with the paste in a wok or very large frying pan over medium–high heat until crispy, around 10 minutes. Set it aside.

Look, sorry vegans – truly. The eggs are optional. But if you are opting to use them – now is the time. Use the same pan as you did the tofu in – just add a lick of peanut oil and then pour in the egg. Swirl the egg pancake over medium heat until just set, about 2 minutes. Remove from the pan, roll up the egg pancake and roughly chop. Set aside also.

Pan-fry the mushrooms in the reserved peanut oil over high heat until the edges are golden brown, around 5 minutes, then add the garlic chives and fry for a further 1 minute.

Add the shredded wombok, noodles and half the sauce to the pan. Carefully toss together.

Add back in the tofu and egg (if using). Toss well.

Serve in a large bowl with the remaining sauce drizzled over the top and lots of bean sprouts, coriander leaves, chopped peanuts and lime wedges.

This is gooooooood!

Serves 4

Lady &
The Tramp

The origin story for this
is both G & M rated.

3 tablespoons Bready Pesto
   from page 216
2 tablespoons extra virgin olive oil,
   for frying

PICI DOUGH*
2 cups (300 g) tipo 00 flour
⅔ cup (170 ml) warm water
3 tablespoons extra virgin olive oil

KALAMATA SALSA
½ cup (75 g) pitted kalamata
   olives, coarsely chopped

2 tablespoons baby capers,
   coarsely chopped
¼ cup (5 g) parsley leaves,
   coarsely chopped
2 tablespoons finely grated
   lemon zest
1 tablespoon red wine vinegar

OPTIONAL INGREDIENTS
a lover to suck the other end
of your noodle

Poor man's bolognese, puttanesca sauce and peasant's pasta: three incredible flavours and textures created in Italy during extremely hard and fast times.

Each of these recipes has its own history but what they all have in common is that they are made from basic, cheap pantry ingredients.

The name Lady and the Tramp hints at the origin story of puttanesca – and the fact that it is so delightfully slurpable, you will be hoping to end a single mouthful with an accidental kiss, just like in the Disney classic.

To make the pici dough, combine the flour, warm water and olive oil in a standmixer fitted with the dough hook on medium speed for 2 minutes, or until the dough has come together. Turn out onto a lightly floured surface and knead for 4–5 minutes, until smooth. Cover in plastic wrap and rest for 30 minutes.

Make the Bready Pesto from page 216 and set aside.

To make the kalamata salsa,

combine the olives, capers and parsley in a small bowl with the lemon zest and red wine vinegar. Set aside also.

Cut small sections of the pasta dough at a time and roll them into long thin strands on a very lightly floured surface. (It actually helps if there's not too much flour on the benchtop when you are rolling.) The beauty of this pasta is it is irregular: thicker in some bits, thinner in others. This is a perfect pasta to get your kids to help with.

Place the rolled pasta onto a lightly floured tray and cover with a tea towel until ready to cook.

The next bit comes together relatively quickly, with fresh pasta and a flash-in-the-pan style sauce. It's a good idea to have everything ready to go before anything goes in the pan.

The pasta should be cooked in a large pot of heavily salted boiling water, and will only take 30 seconds to 1 minute.

Meanwhile, in a large deep frying pan, heat 2 tablespoons of olive oil over medium–high heat. Add the

bready pesto and heat it through until aromatic, 1 minute or so. Use tongs to add the pasta straight from the boiling water into the pan with the pesto and toss to coat. Add about ½ cup (125 ml) of pasta water to loosen the sauce and toss to combine.

Serve immediately topped with the kalamata salsa.

* Replace the pici dough with store-bought spaghetti and premake the pesto & salsa and you're 10 minutes from door to dinner glory!

Serves 4

Shortstop Bowls

A rolling boil. Heavily salted. A flash in the pan. A blitz of flavours.
A stir of textures. A shower of parmy. And a scrunch of pepper.
Very fast. Very easy. Very delicious. Weeknight pasta hacks for snack attacks.
MEMO! Always keep a scoop of pasta water, always drizzle with olive oil.

Serves 4

Angel Hair & Tomato Sunshine

5 large ripe tomatoes
1 garlic clove, smashed
1 shallot, finely chopped
1 teaspoon sea salt flakes
1 teaspoon white
  (granulated) sugar
¼ cup (7 g) loosely packed
  basil leaves, chopped
1 tablespoon red wine vinegar
¼ cup (60 ml) extra virgin olive oil
500 g (1 lb 2 oz) angel hair pasta
¼ cup (25 g) finely grated
  parmesan

Cut the toms in half and grate the flesh into a bowl. Macerate with all that other good stuff: garlic, shallot, salt, sugar, basil, red wine vinegar and olive oil.

Cook the pasta, then toss through the toms and tons of cheese.

Burnt Broc Mac 'n' Cheese

4 cups (240 g) broccoli florets
2 tablespoons extra virgin olive oil
500 g (1 lb 2 oz) macaroni
¼ cup (60 g) salted butter, cubed
2 cups (200 g) grated cheddar
1 cup (230 g) cream cheese,
  cubed
1 teaspoon fine salt

Preheat the oven to 220°C (425°F) fan-forced. Toss the broccoli in oil and bake it on a baking paper-lined baking tray for 15 minutes.

Cook and drain the macaroni.

Melt the butter in the empty pasta pot, add the cheddar, cream cheese, pasta, salt and broccoli and stir well.

Herby Chunk Pesto

1 cup (140 g) frozen or fresh peas
1 cup (155 g) frozen broad beans
1 garlic clove, coarsely chopped
¼ cup (5 g) mint leaves
¼ cup (15 g) dill
¼ cup (5 g) parsley leaves
½ cup (50 g) finely grated
  parmesan
¼ cup (60 ml) extra virgin olive oil
500 g (1 lb 2 oz) horseshoe pasta
  (or any short pasta shape)
½ cup (100 g) goat's curd
1 pinch of chilli flakes (optional)

Place the thawed peas and beans in a small bowl with the garlic, herbs, parmesan and oil. Use a stick blender or food processor to blitz the mixture until the desired texture is achieved.

Cook the pasta, then stir through the pesto with a bit of the pasta water. Top with goat's curd (and chilli if you want).

I like my Tuesdays with a little less effort but still a lot of impact.

Take whatever straps you wore to be 'official' off for the day – ties, bras, belts, helmets, mascara all included – pour yourself a long glass of tea – long island or herbal – and let's do big bulky flavours with a pretty laid-back attitude.

The concept here is: avoid the stovetop altogether or cut down on pan count.

Take some time to answer the 'socks' question (see page 7).

I don't know about you, but for me, Tuesday often presents me with about as much energy as a gumboot full of water. The weekend was a century ago and an infinity ahead. Today seems like the day everything is overdue. Let it win. Forfeiting is my new power move.

Toned-down Tuesdays

Ultra Ratta Tarte Tatin

Kinda ratatouille without the sophisticated stacking.

2 tablespoons extra virgin olive oil
1 zucchini (courgette), cut into
   5 mm (¼ inch) rounds
1 brown onion, cut into thin rings
1 eggplant (aubergine), cut into
   1 cm (½ inch) rounds
2 tomatoes, cut into
   5 mm (¼ inch) rounds
fine salt and freshly ground
   black pepper, to season
230 g (8½ oz) fresh ricotta
   (the deli kind in a basket)
½ cup (50 g) grated cheddar

2 tablespoons finely grated
   lemon zest
1 garlic clove, smashed
¼ cup (60 g) basil pesto
   (store-bought is fine)
2 sheets ready-made frozen
   puff pastry, cut into 30 cm
   (12 inch) rounds
small handful of basil leaves,
   to sprinkle on top

OPTIONAL INGREDIENTS
obedience & basil leaves

Ultra. Ratta. Tarte. Tatin.

Sounds exactly like an 80s frat or sorority house.

Although there is no hazing on this guy, the beauty of the layering is that you don't need to stress about the size of the veg all matching so you can create that perfect layered effect of overlapping circles.

Preheat the oven to 180°C (350°F) fan-forced. Grease a 28 cm (11¼ inch) non-stick ovenproof frying pan with 1 tablespoon of the olive oil.

Layer the zucchini in the pan first, then the onion, eggplant and tomatoes – seasoning each layer with S+P as you go.

Drizzle with another tablespoon of olive oil and bake for 20 minutes. Remove the pan from the oven and add 2 tablespoons water, then return it to the oven for a further 10 minutes.

Remove from the oven and allow to cool slightly in the pan, around 10 minutes.

Increase the oven temperature to 250°C (480°F) fan-forced.

Combine the ricotta, cheddar, lemon zest, garlic and pesto in a medium bowl.

Spoon the ricotta mixture on top of the tomatoes, leaving a 2 cm (¾ inch) bare edge around the circumference to tuck the pastry into.

Place both the pastry sheets on top of the cheese and tuck in at the sides. This will give you an extra crispy layered puff. If you can get your hands on some home-made or really thick puff, then you'll only need one layer.

Pop the pan back in the oven and bake for 15–20 minutes, watching carefully for puffy perfect crispness. Rotate the pan if there is a hotspot and any areas are getting too dark.

This next step is pretty daring: let the pan cool slightly to avoid anything too hot and too dangerous, then flip the pan straight onto your serving plate.

You can decorate with a few flicky little basil leaves.

Cut into wedges to serve.

Serves 4

Bombay Wish Potatoes

I've never been to Mumbai
but I've been to me.

1 tablespoon extra virgin olive oil

FLATTIES
1⅔ cups (250 g) wholemeal (whole-wheat) self-raising flour, plus a little extra for rolling
1 cup (260 g) Greek-style yoghurt
1 teaspoon fine salt
2 teaspoons extra virgin olive oil
¼ cup (30 g) chopped spring onion (scallion), white and green parts

POTATOES
¼ cup (60 ml) ghee, melted
1 red onion, thinly sliced
2 garlic cloves, smashed
30 curry leaves
½ teaspoon turmeric powder
1 teaspoon brown mustard seeds
1 teaspoon white mustard seeds
2 teaspoons curry powder
½ teaspoon fine salt
1 big head broccoli, trimmed and cut into florets
1 kg (2 lb 4 oz) potatoes, cut into 1 x 3 cm (½ x 1¼ inch) chunks, skins on

CHUTNEY
2 cups (60 g) coriander (cilantro) leaves
1 cup (20 g) mint leaves
1 tablespoon finely grated fresh ginger
3 garlic cloves
2 teaspoons cumin powder
1 teaspoon fine salt
1 teaspoon white (granulated) sugar
1 tablespoon lime juice

OPTIONAL INGREDIENTS
yoghurt, coriander and lime and rosé

This baby's namesake is making me wish I was in Mumbai – but now that I've said it out loud it may not come true.

Crispy flatties, chewy potatoes and an intensely flavoured classic Indian green chutney: this dish is kind of like an inside-out rustic dosa or a deconstructed aloo paratha. Which I am FINE with.

It's an incredible medley of flavours and textures that makes for a truly enjoyable eating experience.

Preheat the oven to 220°C (425°F). Line a baking tray with baking paper.

Place all the flatty dough ingredients in the bowl of a standmixer fitted with the dough hook and mix on medium speed until well combined. Turn down to low and continue mixing for 10 minutes. Set aside covered in a warm place for an hour to rest. It may rise a bit but that's not essential so don't worry – sometimes the wholemeal weighs it (and everything) down.

For the potatoes, place the ghee, onion, garlic, curry leaves and spices into a large bowl and mix to combine.* Add in the broccoli and potato and mix well. Scatter on the baking tray and bake for 25 minutes, or until the potatoes are crispy on the edges and soft in the middle.

Meanwhile, for the chutney, simply blend all the ingredients plus 2 tablespoons of water in a food processor until the mixture is emulsified and smooth. The quantity is more than you will need but it's so delicious you will be happy for leftovers! Store leftover chutney in a jar in the fridge for up to 1 week or freeze for later days.

Roll out handfuls of flatty dough on a lightly floured surface and pan-fry in a non-stick frying pan with the olive oil over medium heat. They should take around 3 minutes each side and be golden and slightly charred when done. Keep warm until serving.

Serve everything together so each person can build their own plate of perfection.

---

* Use a spoon or kitchen gloves so you don't stain yourself yellow.

Serves 4 as a snack or side

¼ cup (70 g) white miso paste
2 garlic cloves, crushed
¼ cup (60 ml) honey
2 tablespoons soy sauce
2 tablespoons rice vinegar
2 teaspoons sesame oil
2 spring onions (scallions),
   finely chopped, whites and
   greens separated
8 cm piece of ginger, peeled
   and julienned
1 large cauliflower, cut into
   8 wedges*

3 tablespoons extra virgin olive oil
2 cups (440 g) white rice
½ teaspoon Chinese five-spice
½ teaspoon fine salt
1 teaspoon sesame seeds

OPTIONAL INGREDIENTS
blanched greens and Chilli Crisp
from page 215

The sticky, chewy business of baking rice with flavours is with us to stay, my friends.

It's a classic lazy approach disguised as a big flavour move. (It's actually both!) And so satisfying, because it's basically set and forget.

Cauliflowers are the greatest sauce-trappers, too.

Preheat the oven to 200°C (400°F) fan-forced.

Blend the miso, garlic, honey, soy, rice vinegar, sesame oil, spring onions (white parts only) and a quarter of the ginger in a food processor until smooth.

Toss the cauliflower through this mix, making sure to coat it really well.

In a large roasting tray big enough to fit the cauliflower in a single layer, combine the olive oil, rice, remaining ginger, Chinese five-spice and salt.

Cover with 3 cups (750 ml) of water and gently shake the pan to level out the rice.

Place the cauliflower into the water, then cover tightly with foil.

Bake for 20 minutes, then uncover and bake for a further 25 minutes, basting with any remaining marinade for the final 5 minutes.

Serve with sesame seeds and the green parts of the spring onions.

---

* Cauliflower can take a while to roast. If you're short on time, blanch (4 minutes), steam (10 minutes) or microwave (4 minutes) the pieces prior to tossing them in the sauce.

Serves 4

Honey Soy Cauli

When cauliflower is not being 'rice' for paleos, it can be 'chicken' for vegos.

Pizza Rice

Oh hey there, covergirl. All the flavours of a vegetarian supreme baked into crispy, chewy rice.

½ red onion, thinly sliced
3 garlic cloves, thinly sliced
⅓ cup (80 ml) extra virgin olive oil,
   plus extra for drizzling
4 button mushrooms, thinly sliced
2 teaspoons dried oregano
½ cup (80 g) pitted black Spanish
   olives, thinly sliced
1–2 roasted marinated red
   capsicums (peppers),
   thinly sliced

2 marinated long-stem artichokes
   (or 4 short-stem), halved
1 teaspoon fine salt
¼ cup (60 g) salted butter
2 cups (440 g) arborio rice
200 g (7 oz) tomato passata
   (puréed tomatoes)
1 punnet cherry tomatoes
   or 2 small trusses of baby
   truss tomatoes
fine salt, to season

¾ cup (105 g) sliced mozzarella
1 burrata, torn
½ cup (50 g) finely grated
   parmesan, for sprinkling
50 g (1¾ oz) rocket (arugula)
small handful of basil leaves

OPTIONAL INGREDIENTS
chilli flakes

**Trust me, rice can feel like pizza.
I am completely about this dish
– it has it all. Great flavour, chewy
textures and a one-pot situation
so proud it's basically gloating.**

**There's pretty much nothing
better.**

Preheat the oven to 180°C (350°F)
fan-forced.

In a large ovenproof frying pan,
sauté the onion and garlic in
the olive oil over medium–high
heat for 2 minutes, until starting
to soften. Add the mushrooms,
oregano, olives, capsicum,
artichoke and 1 teaspoon of salt
and fry for a further 1 minute.
Add the butter and arborio rice,
reduce the heat to medium and
stir well to coat the rice in the
butter and pan flavours.

Add the passata and about 600 ml
(21 fl oz) of water.

Top with cherry tomatoes (or baby
truss). Drizzle with 1 tablespoon
olive oil and sprinkle with salt
to season.

Place the pan in the oven. After
25 minutes, remove the pan from
the oven and top with sliced
mozzarella and a drizzle of olive oil.
Return the pan to the oven to cook
for a further 10 minutes, until the
cheese is melted and bubbling.

Top with torn burrata, parmesan,
rocket and basil when serving.

Serves 4

90s Scissor Slice

The anti-prove pizza is a lack-
of-patience best friend.

1 tablespoon extra virgin olive oil
2 teaspoons semolina, for dusting
125 g (4½ oz) mozzarella
130 g (4½ oz) tomato passata
(puréed tomatoes)
1 handful baby rocket leaves

MUSHROOM TOPPING
2 cups (180 g) sliced mushrooms
(field, Swiss and button are
all great – if you want cheap
authenticity then just do
the button)
1 garlic clove, smashed
2 tablespoons white wine vinegar
1 teaspoon fine salt
¼ cup (60 ml) extra virgin olive oil
½ cup (30 g) finely chopped
curly parsley

PIZZA DOUGH
3 cups (450 g) plain
(all-purpose) flour
1 teaspoon instant yeast
¾ cup (185 ml) lukewarm water
2 tablespoons extra virgin olive oil
1 teaspoon fine salt
¼ teaspoon white
(granulated) sugar

OPTIONAL INGREDIENTS
chilli flakes & cigarettes

In the 90s, these were floppy, oily & super thin metre-long pizzas. They could be scissor-cut to order from the counter in 15 cm (6 inch) sections, skimmed with cheese and sparingly placed but delicious toppings.

The 90s food m.o. was 'height equals flavour'. These were Calvin Klein-esque by comparison – until you ate five.

Combine the mushroom topping ingredients and allow to marinate for half an hour. Resist eating as is.

Preheat the oven to 240°C (475°F) fan-forced. Oil your two largest baking trays and dust them with semolina.

Grate the mozz and set aside.*

Combine the dough ingredients until smooth and elastic (by hand or standmixer). Don't let it rise! (Key component of the 'less time is better value' motto for recipes around here.)

Divide the dough in half and roll out two thin rectangles to fit the trays.

Divide the passata between the two pizzas and brush right to the edges (yes!). Divide the mozz between both and top with evenly scattered 'shrooms.

(If this were another book I'd 100% add anchovies here but don't worry, I'm not even going to mention it.)

Bake until bubbling on top and the crust is cooked, around 15 minutes. Top each pizza with the rocket leaves.

* Hot tip: freeze the mozzarella for 5 minutes before grating to make it less like grating a silicone breast implant (guessing here).

**Makes two 30 x 40 cm
(12 x 16 inch) pizzas**

500 g (1 lb 2 oz) corn chips
1 corn cob, kernels removed,
    covered with boiling water
    for 5 minutes, then drained
1 tablespoon extra virgin olive oil,
    for drizzling

NACHO SAUCE
½ brown onion, finely diced
1 tablespoon extra virgin olive oil
3 garlic cloves, smashed
1 celery stalk, finely chopped
2 tablespoons Mexican Seasoning
    from page 216
1 tablespoon chipotle in adobo
400 g (14 oz) tinned black beans
400 g (14 oz) tinned refried beans
1 tablespoon tomato paste
    (concentrated purée)

SMOKED CHEESE SAUCE
2 tablespoons salted butter
1½ tablespoons plain
    (all-purpose) flour
2 cups (500 ml) milk
3 cups (300 g) grated
    smoked cheddar
250 g (9 oz) tinned creamed corn

SALSA
2 roma tomatoes, seeds removed,
    flesh diced
1 jalapeño, thinly sliced
1 small red onion, finely diced
large handful coriander (cilantro)
    leaves, chopped
sea salt flakes and freshly ground
    black pepper, to taste

DRIZZLE
1 cup (245 g) sour cream
2 tablespoons lime juice
1 tablespoon extra virgin olive oil
1 tablespoon hot water

OPTIONAL INGREDIENTS
in my house 3/5 people hate avos,
so I only add them when feeling
spiteful – but this would go so well
with a good guac

I realise the reason I don't often want to eat nachos is that I get full while cooking, but that doesn't stop the desire for this scoopable snack situation. So damn good.

Preheat the oven to 200°C (400°F) fan-forced.

First, make the nacho sauce. Sweat the onion over medium heat in a large frying pan with olive oil for 5 minutes. Add the garlic, celery and spice mix and fry for a further 5 minutes. Add the chipotle, black beans (don't drain), the refried beans and tomato paste. Sauté for 10 minutes, then add ½ cup (125 ml) of water and simmer until reduced – a further 10 minutes. Set aside.

For the cheese sauce, in a medium saucepan over medium heat, melt the butter, then stir in the flour to form a smooth golden paste.

Cook for 2 minutes, then add the milk and whisk until smooth. Add the smoked cheese and creamed corn and cook until thick and the cheese has melted, around 8 minutes. Set this aside.

For the salsa, toss together the tomatoes, jalapeño, red onion and coriander leaves in a small bowl. Season with S+P.

In the base of a 30 x 40 cm (12 x 16 inch) ovenproof dish, place alternating spoonfuls of the nacho and cheese sauces, using about half of each. Nestle corn chips vertically into this, then fill the gaps with the remaining nacho and cheese sauce.

Scatter the corn kernels about and then drizzle the whole thing with olive oil.

Bake for 15 minutes, until the chips are toasted and the filling is hot.

Meanwhile, combine the sour cream, lime juice, olive oil and hot water in a bowl and mix well.

Straight out of the oven, dribble the salsa and sour cream mixture on top. Eat from the tray.

Serves 4

Nachos Mess

Being beautiful **and** a
sloppy bog is possible.

Only Sides

All the bits and pieces for a perfect
roast dinner – hold the hero, thanks.

2 kg (4 lb 8 oz) unwashed
  potatoes, peeled and quartered
2 parsnips, peeled and halved
  lengthways
2 apples, halved across the middle
1 tablespoon lemon juice
90 ml (3 fl oz) honey
4 carrots, cut diagonally into
  5 cm (2 inch) chunks
1 brown onion

250 g (9 oz) green beans,
  tops removed
1 cup (130 g) frozen baby peas
2 tablespoons rice bran oil
⅓ cup (90 g) salted butter
¼ cup (60 ml) milk
fine salt and freshly ground
  black pepper, to taste
½ bunch thyme sprigs
¼ kent pumpkin (squash), skin
  on and seeds removed, cut into
  3 cm (1¼ inch) wedges

1 head garlic, root end cut off,
  skin left on
4 rosemary sprigs
1 cup (250 ml) gravy* from
  page 113

OPTIONAL INGREDIENTS
wholegrain mustard

Quite frankly, there is very little room in the oven (or time or energy) for meat in this recipe anyway.

It's the OnlyFans version of a big roast: it's OnlySides.

Preheat the oven to 200°C (400°F) fan-forced.

Soak half the potatoes in cold water to remove some of the starch while you prepare the other veg.

Put the parsnip and apple in a bowl with 1 cup (250 ml) of water, lemon juice and 1 tablespoon of the honey.

To peel or not to peel carrots? That is the question. Either way is great, but your enthusiasm will help you decide.

Cut the onion into 1 cm (½ inch) rings with the skin on (be careful, it's slippery!), then just remove the outer ring and voila! It is peeled.

Place the beans and peas in a heatproof bowl ready for blanching.

Now that your veggies are prepped, it's a time game – everything has its own needs.

Dry the soaking spuds, then toss them in 1 tablespoon of the rice bran oil, place them on a large

shallow-sided tray and roast them for 20 minutes.

Boil the remaining potatoes in plenty of salted water until soft – 20 minutes – then drain in a colander. Place the pot back on the stove on medium heat with half of the butter and the milk. Once the butter is melted add the spuds back in and mash well. Season to taste, cover and keep warm until serving (you may need to reheat with a bit more milk and butter later).

Melt the remaining butter and honey together in a small saucepan. Line a second tray with baking paper and place the parsnips, onion rings, apples and thyme on the tray. Cover with honey butter and 1 tablespoon of the lemon water. Toss well. Season with salt and pepper. Position the apples face up.

Toss the carrots and pumpkin in the remaining rice bran oil.

Turn the oven down to 180°C (350°F) fan-forced and place the tray of parsnips and so on in the oven. At the same time add the carrots, pumpkin, garlic (cut side down) and rosemary to the potato tray.

Roast for a further 30 minutes, checking and turning the veg (turn the apples face down) after 15 minutes.

Meanwhile, blanch the beans and peas by pouring freshly boiled water over them and letting them sit for 5 minutes. Drain and season with salt and butter to taste.

Heat the gravy and reheat the mash if necessary before serving.

---

* Make the gravy ahead of time and freeze. Defrost in the fridge overnight and reheat on a whim (in a small saucepan over medium heat, stirring, for 10 minutes).

Serves 4

Stacked Eggplant Parm

A lava-like tray of heaven.

2 eggplants (aubergine)
2 teaspoons sea salt flakes
2 tablespoons extra virgin olive oil
260 g (9¼ oz) tomato passata
   (puréed tomatoes)
400 g (14 oz) tinned
   cherry tomatoes
3 garlic cloves, crushed
¾ cup (45 g) panko breadcrumbs
¼ cup (25 g) grated parmesan
1 tablespoon dried oregano
1 tablespoon finely grated
   lemon zest

1 brown onion, sliced
100 g (3½ oz) fresh buffalo
   mozzarella in water, sliced
100 g (3½ oz) mozzarella, sliced

GNOCCHI
1 tablespoon extra virgin olive oil
500 g (1 lb 2 oz) frozen
   potato gnocchi

OPTIONAL
chilli if you're into it

When someone tags #squadgoals, your mind might flit to model-esque 'you can't sit with us' types. Me? I think of fat-belly beauties: the Venus of Willendorf, mozzarella and eggplant.

I'm going to ask you to use two pans in this recipe, but I promise it's low-key cooking. Low key and lazy and resulting in soft, sweet eggplant, rich and tangy toms, molten golden cheese and chewy potato gems.

That's hot.

Preheat the oven to 200°C (400°F) fan-forced.

Slice the eggplants in half lengthways and score with slits 1 cm (½ inch) apart diagonally across the face. Season with half of the salt.

Brush a baking dish with half of the olive oil and place the eggplants cut-side down onto the dish.

Bake for 15 minutes, until the skin has begun to wrinkle and the flesh is soft.

Meanwhile, combine the passata, cherry tomatoes, 200 ml (7 fl oz) water, half the garlic and all the remaining salt in a bowl.

In a separate bowl, combine the panko, parmesan, remaining garlic, oregano and lemon zest. Set aside.

Remove the eggplants from the dish and set aside.

Brush the remaining oil into the dish then place the sliced onion around the dish. Top with the passata mixture then nestle the eggplants back in, this time cut-side up.

Return to the oven for 15 minutes, until the tomatoes begin to bubble around the edges.

Remove the dish from the oven.

Sprinkle the eggplant evenly with the panko crumb mixture and top with the sliced cheeses, alternating between them.

Scoop a little bit of the tomato mixture up onto the cheese, then return the dish to the oven for 10 minutes, until golden and bubbling.

Meanwhile, cook the gnocchi.

Heat the oil over medium–high heat in a large non-stick frying pan with a lid.

Place the still frozen gnocchi in a single layer into the pan. Add 2 tablespoons of water and cover.

Cook for 10 minutes, until golden brown on the outside and fluffy on the inside: like perfect little chewy potato gems.

Serve the eggplant with a spoonful of gnocchi and plenty of sauce scooped from the tray.

Serves 4

Personality Potatoes

Spud, tater, chip, crisp, mash, fries, roasties, gratin.
Soft, fluffy, crunchy, crispy, gooey, creamy, golden, smooth, chewy.
I mean, when are they NOT great?
Eat these whenever you like.

Serves 4–6 as a side

Sticky

1 kg (2 lb 4 oz) red spuds,
    skins on, cut into chunks
1 garlic clove, smashed
2 tablespoons extra virgin olive oil
2 cups (500 ml) vegetable stock
1 teaspoon paprika
¼ cup (60 g) salted butter, sliced

Preheat the oven to 200°C (400°F)
fan-forced.

In an ovenproof frying pan over
medium heat sauté the spuds
and garlic in olive oil for 5 minutes,
until the garlic begins to go
golden.

Add the stock and paprika and
reduce the heat to a simmer
for 20 minutes.

Remove from the heat, place
butter on top and bake in the
oven for a further 20 minutes,
until golden brown and all the
liquid has evaporated.

Loaded

1 kg (2 lb 4 oz) yellow-flesh variety
    spuds, peeled and halved
½ cup (100 g) frozen spinach,
    thawed
1 zucchini (courgette), grated
2 tablespoons single (pure) cream
⅓ cup (90 g) salted butter,
    chopped
1 cup (125 g) grated mozzarella
fine salt and freshly ground black
    pepper, to taste

Preheat the oven to 200°C (400°F)
fan-forced.

Boil the potatoes in plenty of
salted water until soft, around
20–25 minutes. Drain and place
back in the pot. Add the spinach
and zucchini and roughly mash
with the cream.

Add the butter and mozzarella
and stir through. Taste and season
well with S+P as desired. Place in
a greased ovenproof dish and
bake until it's crispy on top and
the cheese has melted, around
20 minutes.

Crispy

1 tablespoon extra virgin olive oil
1 kg (2 lb 4 oz) cocktail spuds,
    halved
1 head garlic, cut in half with
    skin left on
1 teaspoon fine salt
2 tablespoons rice bran oil
1 tablespoon polenta
1 cup (100 g) finely grated
    parmesan

Preheat the oven to 200°C (400°F)
fan-forced. Lightly grease a
baking tray with olive oil.

Place the spuds, garlic and salt
in a pot of cold water and bring
to the boil. Boil for 15 minutes.

Drain and place the spuds back
into the pot on low heat to dry.
Add the rice bran oil and cover,
then shake the pot vigorously.

Tip everything onto the baking
tray and squash the spuds flat
slightly with a spatula.

Sprinkle with polenta and
parmesan.

Roast for 30 minutes, until
crisp and golden brown.

Soooooooooop.

This is possibly my favourite chapter: noodle soup, thick soup, creamy or brothy, loaded with veg, summer soup, breakfast soup, winter soup, midnight soup ... soup has no time-zone or season. There is barely a day that soup is not a welcome addition to my life.

But maybe I like it most because you have to concentrate while you eat it. You forage for chunks of veg, scoop and swirl creamy toppings, catch crispy bits and navigate the journey from bowl to face with care.

Soup is the best! You'll also find general wet bowl food here.

#S4L (Soup4Life)

Saucy
Wet
Wednesdays

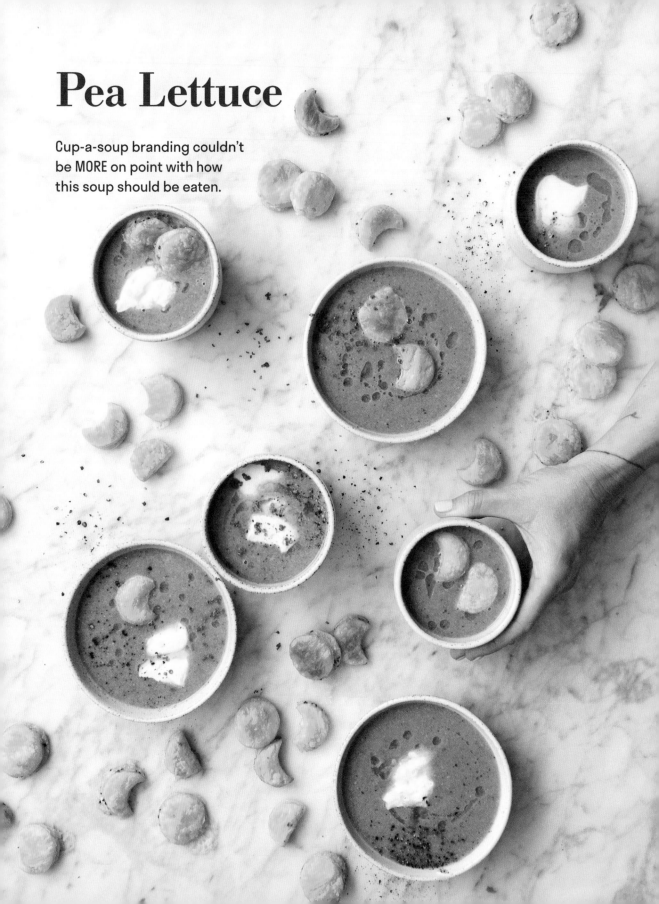

Pea Lettuce

Cup-a-soup branding couldn't be MORE on point with how this soup should be eaten.

1 leek
2 sheets ready-made
  frozen shortcrust pastry
1½ cups (150 g) grated cheddar
¼ cup (15 g) finely snipped chives
2 garlic cloves, chopped
¼ cup (60 g) salted butter
½ cup (10 g) flat-leaf
  parsley leaves
1 large iceberg (or any other)
  lettuce, coarsely chopped
6 cups (800 g) frozen baby peas

1.5 litres (6 cups) vegetable stock
fine salt and freshly ground black
  pepper, to taste

OPTIONAL INGREDIENTS
icebergs of sour cream

When my Aunt Sal first told me about this recipe I thought she was nuts.

Cooked lettuce. Blerk.

But it sounded simple enough and appealed to my dreams of one day living like I mean it: wearing velour and sipping soup from a martini glass.

So I made it. And I liked it.

Preheat the oven to 180°C (350°F) fan-forced. Line a baking tray with baking paper.

Jump forward to the leek for a second. To really rinse the leek, trim the tough green ends off and discard, then make a slice from the top of the leek well down past the point where the leaves turn white. Rotate the leek and repeat the cut on the other side. Feather the leaves out and place top down in a jug of water. The ends will open up and grit should fall out. Let the leek soak while you make cute crackers.

Lay one sheet of shortcrust on baking paper. Sprinkle the cheddar and chives on top, then place the second pastry sheet on top of that. Cover this with baking paper and press down evenly (but not too heavily).

Remove the top layer of baking paper and cut the pastry into ridiculously adorable shapes with a cookie cutter. I made the moon phases.

Bake until golden, around 15 minutes. The crackers will keep stored in an airtight container at room temperature for a few days.

Back to that leek – drain and roughly chop.

In a large stockpot, over low heat, sweat the leek and garlic in the butter with the lid on until soft and sweet. This will take around 15 minutes but check and stir occasionally so nothing burns.

Add the parsley, lettuce, peas and stock. Bring to simmering point.

Let it simmer for 15 minutes with the lid ajar, until everything is wilted and cooked.

Using a stick blender, purée the soup to the desired chunkiness. I like mine smooth-ish. Season with salt and pepper and serve with the cute crackers.

Serves 4

Potato Bread Soup

Potato and wafer should have a portmanteau like potafer. Or we can just call it a raw crisp.

4 cups stale bread,
    torn into chunks
½ cup (125 ml) extra virgin olive oil
fine salt, to season
6 garlic cloves, sliced
1–2 long red chillies, finely sliced
2 litres (8 cups) vegetable stock
280 g (10 oz) potatoes, sliced into
    3 mm (⅛ inch) wafers
sea salt flakes, to taste
120 g (4½ oz) baby rocket
    (arugula)
2 teaspoons chilli oil

OPTIONAL INGREDIENTS
you certainly don't need a cold
to enjoy this

We can blame another matriarch in my family – my godmother Kyrsty – for this one.

She brought it to me once when I had the flu – just a regular flu; an elevated cold, shall we say.

Again, the concept seemed weird (see lettuce soup on previous page), but actually – salty, garlicky, chilli broth, with 2 x carbs AND peppery rocket? It just works. Google 'potato bread soup' and all you'll find are lumpy anaemic pots of glug that instantly make you feel as if you'll forever talk like you do actually have tonsillitis. This is NOT that.

Preheat the oven to 180°C (350°F) fan-forced. Line a baking tray with baking paper.

In a bowl, toss the bread chunks in 2 tablespoons of the olive oil and season with salt.

Bake on the tray until golden, turning once, around 15 minutes all up. Allow to cool (you can store in an airtight container at room temperature for up to a week).

Heat the remaining olive oil over high heat in a stockpot. Add the garlic and chilli and fry these until they start to go a lovely dark golden colour and smell strong and bossy, around 4 minutes. Do NOT abandon. You really want that golden flavour, but not burnt.

Straight away add the stock and bring it to a boil.

Turn the heat to medium, add the potato wafers and cook until tender, around 5 minutes.

Season well.

To serve, ladle the soup into bowls, top each with a handful* of croutons, add a handful* of rocket and splash with chilli oil.

---

* Handfuls, in this case, depend entirely on you. You can base it on your actual hand or your hunger.

Serves 4

CONGEE

5 dried shiitake mushrooms
1 cup (250 ml) boiling water
2.5 cm (1 inch) knob of ginger, peeled and julienned
2 garlic cloves
1 celery stalk, chopped
3 spring onions (scallions), white parts chopped, green tops thinly sliced and set aside for topping
1 cup (30 g) loosely packed coriander (cilantro) leaves, stems and roots reserved and washed
¼ cup (60 ml) peanut oil
1 tablespoon sesame oil
1 tablespoon white miso paste
½ cup (110 g) short-grain brown rice
½ cup (110 g) short-grain white rice
fine salt and freshly ground black pepper, to taste
75 g (2½ oz) mushrooms, sliced (I used baby king browns)

SPICY BUBBLES

1 teaspoon Chinese five-spice
½ teaspoon chilli powder
1 teaspoon garlic powder
2 teaspoons crispy fried shallots, crushed
½ teaspoon fine salt
1 cup (30 g) rice bubbles
vegetable oil spray
2 cups (100 g) firmly packed baby spinach leaves

OPTIONAL INGREDIENTS

bamboo shoots and chilli oil; a boiled egg would be fun too

Congee is a condiment carrier and an activity. It's a suspension system. Thick enough to hold a layering of delightful ingredients, but thin enough to warrant spoon-eating. Brown and white rice become the soup, with slippery delicious 'shrooms and snappy little bubbles on the top. Seasoning is essential. Congee is traditionally very basic, usually just cooked with water, but because my family doesn't condiment very well, I am adding a bunch of flavour to the base.

Try any mushroom you'd like in the fresh department. I am using fresh baby king brown – prince browns maybe.

Steep the dried shiitake in the boiling water until cool.

Use a stick blender or food processor to blend the ginger, garlic, celery, the white parts of the spring onion, the stems and roots of the coriander and the peanut oil to form a chunky paste.

Fry the paste over medium heat in a large stockpot, stirring, until it becomes aromatic, around 5 minutes.

Add in the sesame oil and miso and mix well for 2 minutes, until aromatic. Add the brown and white rice and combine.

Drain the shiitake water into the stockpot, then slice the mushrooms and reserve. Add 10 cups (2.5 litres) water and bring to a simmer.

Reduce the heat to low and cook gently, stirring often, for 1–2 hours with the lid ajar, until the rice has completely broken down and become porridge-like. You may need to add more liquid. Taste as you go but season cautiously until the end – then go nuts! Add the mushrooms about half an hour before done or at serving time.

To make the spicy bubbles, combine the Chinese five-spice, chilli powder, garlic powder, fried shallots and salt in a small bowl and mix well. Place the rice bubbles in a large bowl and spray

with oil. Toss well and spray again. Sprinkle the spice mix onto the rice bubbles and continue to toss.

Add the spinach, if using, to the congee 5 minutes before serving, to wilt in the pot. Or – if you like it fresher – just pop the leaves in the bowls before serving and ladle congee on top.

Serve with spicy bubbles, bamboo shoots and chilli oil if using, the tops of the spring onions and the coriander leaves.

Serves 4

Mushroom & Miso Congee

You need to understand texture and condiments to love congee.

Fennel Ragu on Polenta

Embrace the sloppy
wetness of this delight.

RAGU
¼ cup (60 ml) extra virgin olive oil
2 red onions, cut into 1 cm
(½ inch) wedges
1 brown onion, cut into 1 cm
(½ inch) wedges
2 fennel bulbs, cut into 3 cm
(1¼ inch) wedges, tops cut
off and fronds retained
for gremolata
3 garlic cloves, smashed
2 capsicums (peppers),
cut into 5 cm (2 inch) slices
1 teaspoon fennel seeds

2 fresh oregano stems
1 teaspoon fine salt
½ teaspoon white
(granulated) sugar
2 tablespoons malt vinegar
400 g (14 oz) tinned cherry
tomatoes

POLENTA
6 cups (1.5 litres)
chicken-style stock
1 cup (190 g) polenta
1 cup (100 g) finely grated
parmesan, plus extra to serve
¼ cup (60 g) salted butter

GREMOLATA
¼ cup (15 g) finely chopped
curly parsley
1 tablespoon finely grated
lemon zest
1 garlic clove, smashed
1 tablespoon fennel fronds,
finely chopped

OPTIONAL INGREDIENTS
a crusty baguette for final
mopping

This dish is an absolute showstopper, full of delicious sticky braised sweet vegetables sitting on a delightfully creamy bed of polenta with a sprinkling of snappy gremolata and extra parmesan on top.

It's fancy enough to serve to guests with proper cutlery and napkins (and even candles), but it's also comforting enough to eat straight from a bowl on your lap in front of the cold blue light of the telly.

Preheat the oven to 200°C (400°F) fan-forced.

In a heavy-based ovenproof dish that has a lid, heat the olive oil over medium heat and sauté the onions for 5 minutes. Once the onions have had a moment to relax, add in the fennel, garlic, capsicum, fennel seeds, oregano (whole stems), salt and sugar and toss well over the heat.

Pour in the vinegar and toss again. Relocate the dish to the oven and bake with the lid off for 25 minutes.

Remove the dish from the oven, add in the cherry tomatoes, then rinse the tin with ¾ cup (200 ml) of water and pour that in also.

Place the lid on and put the dish back in the oven to bake for another 25 minutes.

Meanwhile, in a large saucepan bring the stock and 2 cups (500 ml) of water to the boil. Whisk in the polenta, pouring it in a steady stream. Keep whisking for 1½–2 minutes so nothing gets stuck on the bottom and there are no lumps. These first minutes are essential to getting very smooth, deliciously creamy polenta. Turn down the heat to medium–low and continue to cook for 25–30 minutes, whisking occasionally. If it seems dry add some more liquid.

To make the gremolata, simply add the ingredients to a little jar or bowl and mix well.

Five minutes before serving, whisk the grated parmesan and butter into the polenta, and keep whisking until smooth and glossy.

Spoon the polenta into a large serving bowl. The polenta will begin to set slightly as it cools.

Top with the steaming sweet braised ragu and sprinkle with gremolata and, of course, extra parmesan.

Serves 4

Summer
Mini

Summer soup. I know.
Do you need to sit down?

1 brown onion, finely diced
2 celery stalks, finely chopped
3 garlic cloves, finely chopped
2 tablespoons extra virgin olive oil,
   plus extra for drizzling
½ cup (110 g) marinated
   artichokes, coarsely chopped
1 zucchini (courgette), sliced
   thinly into rounds
2 teaspoons finely chopped
   fresh oregano leaves
1 small head of broccoli,
   cut into florets*
4 cups (1 litre) chicken-style stock
10 leaves cavolo nero (tuscan
   kale), tough ribs discarded,
   leaves and tender ribs
   kept whole

1¼ cups (60 g) firmly packed
   baby spinach leaves
2 tablespoons finely grated
   parmesan

PESTO
2 tablespoons fresh
   oregano leaves
1 garlic clove, smashed
½ cup (50 g) finely grated
   parmesan
2 tablespoons finely grated
   lemon zest
2 tablespoons pine nuts,
   lightly toasted and cooled
1 tablespoon finely chopped
   dill sprigs

1 tablespoon finely chopped
   flat-leaf parsley
10 basil leaves, torn
1 tablespoon finely chopped
   rosemary leaves
1 cup (130 g) frozen baby peas,
   thawed
½ cup (125 ml) extra virgin olive oil
1 teaspoon sea salt flakes
freshly ground black pepper,
   to taste

OPTIONAL INGREDIENTS
warm summer temps

I've started putting peas in almost every pesto I make at home – it just seems to be a great addition of veg.

This is called a summer mini because it's green and punchy, full of vibrant summer flings, but of course it's really great in winter too. The point of this soup is to remind you that soup has no season and you should eat it anytime.

Roughly blitz all the ingredients for the pesto in a food processor or with a stick blender until you have a rough and chunky consistency. Set aside.

In a large heavy-based saucepan over medium heat, sweat the onion, celery and garlic in olive oil until softened, about 10 minutes. Add the artichokes, zucchini, oregano and the broccoli, increase the heat and fry for a further 2 minutes.

Add the stock and bring to a simmer with the lid ajar. Everything should be tender in about 5 minutes.

Add the cavolo nero and spinach and simmer until wilted, around 2 minutes.

Serve topped with pesto, a drizzle of olive oil and parmy.

---

* Hot tip for cutting broccoli. Hold it upside down over the tray or saucepan you are cooking in and trim the florets off. You may need to cut some in half, and you should skin and julienne the stalk bits too, but doing it this way will result in way less broccoli sand, which is a substantial enough excuse to never use the brassica again.

Serves 4

2 tablespoons extra virgin olive oil
1 red onion, chopped
2 cm (¾ inch) knob of ginger, peeled and grated
4 garlic cloves, chopped
20 curry leaves
2 tablespoons curry powder
2 x 400 g (14 oz) tinned chickpeas, drained
2 carrots, sliced into 1 cm (½ inch) rounds

2 x 400 g (14 oz) tinned crushed tomatoes
6 cups (1.5 litres) vegetable stock
150 g (5½ oz) frozen spinach

OPTIONAL INGREDIENTS
Greek yoghurt, crispy fried shallots, chilli flakes and a squeeze of lime would be nice

Soup is a really strong take-to-work lunch game. For starters, a jar of soup is deceptively filling, but bringing other jars filled with stuff to bulk out your soup OR add flavour is immensely impressive.

It just screams mindfulness and prowess.

Aside from becoming noticeably cooler – eating jar food – you will actually save money by having leftovers for lunch. I know, what a concept! Aaand, if you select your jars correctly, you could even pass your lunch off as something you bought from a super bougie soup/juice cleanse joint.

Clearly this is not me – my jars just say: 'She eats lots of jam.'

This soup is a complete throw together – one worth getting the hang of and putting on when you need.

Heat the oil in a large heavy-based saucepan over medium heat. Add the red onion and sauté for a bit, around 5 minutes.

Add the ginger, garlic, curry leaves and curry powder and sauté for a further 2 minutes.

It should smell great right about now.

Add the drained chickpeas, the carrots (don't even bother to peel – but this is up to you), the crushed toms and the stock. Simmer for 30 minutes with the lid ajar.

Add the frozen spinach, or any green leaves you like, and cook for another 10 minutes or so.

Bulk it out with steamed rice or add any number of accessories from the list above!

Serves 4

Quick & Curried

Forget dressing for success,
lunch for luxury instead.

Sorrel Spinach Soup

Creamy mash IN a bowl of thick soup is a double delight – and it appeals to me far more than having cake and eating it too.

600 g (1 lb 5 oz) potatoes,
  peeled and cubed
100 g (3½ oz) salted butter
½ cup (130 g) natural yoghurt
1 tablespoon extra virgin olive oil
1 small brown onion, finely diced
1 small carrot, finely chopped
2 garlic cloves, finely chopped
1 celery stalk, finely chopped
1 bay leaf
4 cups (1 litre) vegetable stock
6 cups (270 g) firmly packed
  baby spinach leaves

1 bunch sorrel
1 tablespoon plain
  (all-purpose) flour
¼ cup (65 g) sour cream

TOPPINGS
40 g (1½ oz) cold salted butter,
  cut into 4 portions
freshly ground black pepper,
  to serve
2 tablespoons dill sprigs

OPTIONAL INGREDIENTS
poached egg

I am neither French nor Polish – but this sorrel soup heralds from both countries and I was lucky enough to be fed it as a kid.

Although sorrel can be pretty difficult to find in the shops, it grows like a weed if left alone. Get matey with your produce dude or buy some seeds. It is lemony and ultimately amazing.

Sorrel can be swapped out for spinach, but you'll lose the tang of this soup, which is what you come back for. Sorrel also turns murky brown when cooked, but the spinach stays bright, which is nice.

Boil the potatoes in plenty of salted water until soft – 20 minutes – then mash until smooth with 2 tablespoons of the butter and the yoghurt. Set aside and keep warm.

In a large saucepan over medium heat, melt the remaining butter with the olive oil and then sauté the onion, carrot, garlic, celery and bay leaf for about 15 minutes, until golden.

Add in the vegetable stock and simmer for 15 minutes with the lid ajar.

Add the spinach and sorrel and cook until just wilted, around 2 minutes.

Remove the bay leaf and blend the soup with a stick blender until very smooth. You can put the bay leaf back in after blending if you would like to flavour the soup a bit more.

In a small bowl, combine the flour and sour cream until they form a smooth paste. Add a few tablespoons of soup to the paste and mix well. Drop this paste back into the soup and stir through.

Serve the soup with a big dollop of mashed potato topped with a portion of butter, plenty of pepper and dill sprigs to garnish.

The soup is also the perfect partner to a poached egg.

Serves 4

Mulligatawny & a Flatty

This can be the skinny fat soup.

1 large brown onion, finely diced
1 carrot, finely diced
2 celery stalks, finely diced
2 tablespoons extra virgin olive oil
5 cm (2 inch) knob of ginger, peeled and grated
3 garlic cloves, smashed
2 teaspoons curry powder
2 teaspoons turmeric powder
1 teaspoon garam masala
1 small sweet potato, peeled and diced

½ cauliflower, core removed, cut into florets
1 green apple, peeled and grated
1 cup (205 g) red lentils
1 tablespoon vegetable stock powder
drizzle of coconut milk, to serve

FLATTIES
2 cups (300 g) self-raising flour
1 cup (260 g) Greek-style yoghurt
1 tablespoon extra virgin olive oil
1 teaspoon fine salt

¼ teaspoon white (granulated) sugar
1 teaspoon each of cumin seeds, nigella seeds, caraway seeds, sesame seeds

OPTIONAL INGREDIENTS
lime & coriander

Mulligatawny is like a slightly sweeter, slurpier dhal. It's perfect for cooler evenings when you need something a little bit more substantial. It's rich and creamy without being too heavy.

In a heavy-based saucepan over medium–low heat sauté the onion, carrot and celery in olive oil until golden and soft, around 15 minutes.

Add the ginger and garlic and sauté for a further 2 minutes.

Add the curry powder, turmeric and garam masala and stir. Add the sweet potato, cauliflower, apple, lentils, stock and 8 cups (2 litres) water and stir well.

Bring the soup to a boil, then turn the heat down to medium and simmer, with the lid ajar, for 30 minutes or until soft.

To make the flatties, in a large bowl combine the flour, yoghurt, olive oil, salt and sugar until a smooth dough has formed. This can be done with a standmixer fitted with a dough hook or a hand fitted with fingers.

If using a standmixer, combine the ingredients for 2–3 minutes on medium speed, then knead for another 7–8 minutes. If working by hand, mix the dough in the bowl for 4–6 minutes then move it to a lightly floured surface to knead for 5–6 minutes, until smooth and elastic (minimal kneading here as it can overwork the dough).

Lightly oil a large bowl and place the dough in it. Dust the top with some flour before covering the bowl with plastic wrap (the flour will stop the dough sticking to the plastic wrap if it rises that high). Set aside in a warm place to rest for about an hour.

Preheat the oven to 200°C (400°F) fan-forced. Line two baking trays with baking paper.

When you are ready to eat, turn the sticky dough out onto a floured surface and divide it into eight pieces. Smoosh each piece out with your fingertips to make a 12 cm (4½ inch) diameter round. Sprinkle with seeds, then place on the trays and bake for 10 minutes, or until golden and puffy.*

Top each bowl of mulligatawny with a big drizzle of coconut milk and serve with the freshly baked flatties on the side.

---

* These are always best cooked fresh; however, you can freeze the dough. Divide the flattened portions with baking paper to stop them from sticking to each other, then place them in an airtight container or bag and freeze. Thaw before cooking.

Serves 4

GREEN GODDESS SAUCE

50 g (1¾ oz) salted butter
1 tablespoon extra virgin olive oil
1 small onion, diced
3 garlic cloves, chopped
4 cups (180 g) firmly packed baby spinach, rinsed but not dried off too much
2 zucchini (courgettes), grated
⅔ cup (20 g) loosely packed basil leaves
1 tablespoon fresh oregano leaves

RISOTTO

8 cups (2 litres) veg stock
1 lemon, peel cut into four 5 cm (2 inch) strips, juice squeezed, plus extra lemon for zesting
1 tablespoon extra virgin olive oil
2 cups (440 g) arborio rice
1 tablespoon dijon mustard
1 bunch asparagus, ends trimmed, cut diagonally into 1 cm (½ inch) pieces
½ cup (80 g) baby peas
40 g (1½ oz) salted butter
1 cup (100 g) finely grated parmesan

TOPPINGS

90 g (3 oz) d'affinois,* cut into 12 slices
small handful of fresh baby herbs
freshly ground black pepper

OPTIONAL INGREDIENTS

nothing to be added, nothing to be removed

This is the kind of food I need to be eating when my kids are treating me to a rendition of a song they've never learned to sing or playing a tune on an instrument they haven't been taught.

The harmonies in the bowl are perfect and the rice al dente. Creamy, fresh, delicious, tangy – al limone/cacio e pepe vibes.

To make the goddess part of this recipe, in a medium saucepan over medium heat melt the butter and olive oil. Add the onion and garlic and sauté for 5 minutes, until it starts to smell wonderful.

Add the baby spinach, grated zucchini, basil and oregano and stir until it wilts – this should take a further 3 minutes. Turn off the heat. The water that comes out of the spinach should be enough to give this mixture a bit of liquid. Allow it to cool slightly, then purée in a small food processor or with a stick blender. Set aside this insanely incredible sauce until ready to use.

Now, bring the stock to simmering in a covered saucepan then turn it off. This is the liquid you will add to the risotto by the ladleful.

In a large heavy-based saucepan over medium heat, sauté the lemon peel in 1 tablespoon of olive oil for 2 minutes. Add the rice and stir well to coat in oil, reduce the heat to low and begin adding the hot stock ½ cup (125 ml) at a time, stirring after each addition.

The constant stirring is essential for creamy risotto. Continue adding stock only as the last amount is absorbed.

Before you add the last amount of liquid, stir in 2 tablespoons of the lemon juice, and the dijon, asparagus and peas, then the butter and the parmesan. The final splash of liquid will help bring everything together.

The rice should be al dente and collapse flat in its own wetness. You can add water if it requires a bit more cooking, but it will continue to cook once it's removed from the heat.

Serve immediately with a swirl of the green sauce and a slice or two of d'affinois. Add a flourish of fresh baby herbs, a big fat scrunch of pepper and a flick of lemon zest.

Any left-over green goddess can be kept in the fridge for a week in an airtight container.

---

* You can use anything your heart desires here, but I suggest you find a cheese that wants to be both cream and butter. Fancy, but without any willpower.

Serves 6

Spring Goddess Risotto

Even if you don't like the people,
you'd turn up for this one.

Thick & Delicious

We all have that one friend.

1 leek
1 brown onion, chopped
2 celery stalks, chopped
3 garlic cloves, chopped
2 tablespoons extra virgin olive oil
400 g (14 oz) potatoes, peeled
 and cut into 4 cm cubes
1 celeriac, peeled and cut into
 4 cm cubes
2 corn cobs, kernels removed
 and cobs reserved (husks and
 silks discarded)

4 cups (1 litre) vegetable stock
1 cup (250 ml) single (pure) cream
¼ cup (15 g) finely snipped chives

OPTIONAL INGREDIENTS
a splash of extra cream

**A velvety chowder so smooth
I'd consider wearing it.**

**Thick & Delicious is full of corn,
potato, leek and that maniac of
a vegetable: celeriac. It's such a
prehistoric looking thing! Falls
firmly into the pile of 'Who the
f*ck decided to eat this first?!'
It's witchy ugly, but so sweet
and delicious.**

**Adding the stripped corn cobs
will give you the best corny
flavour, so keep them simmering
with everything else until the last
moment, then get rid of them.**

After you've washed your leek (see
page 59), cut 10 cm off the green
end and julienne it. Pat dry and set
aside. Cut the remaining leek into
1 cm (½ inch) rounds.

In a large saucepan over low
heat, sauté the onion, celery, leek
rounds and garlic in half the olive
oil for 10 minutes with the lid on.

Add in the potato, celeriac and
corn cobs (no, not the kernels yet!)
and cover with the stock. Simmer
with the lid ajar until the veg has
softened, around 25 minutes.

Remove the corn cobs, add in
half of the kernels and cook for
a further 5 minutes.

Purée the soup with a stick
blender until smooth.

Add the remaining corn kernels
and the cream and simmer for
5 minutes.

Meanwhile, in a shallow non-stick
frying pan, heat the remaining
olive oil and fry the julienned leeks
until golden brown and beginning
to crisp, around 5 minutes. Place
on paper towel to drain.

Eat this thick and delicious
situation with a little flurry of leek
crisps and a caviar of chives.

Serves 4

Canned Bread Soup

Involves holding bread, and also scooping bread.

2 tablespoons extra virgin olive oil, plus extra for drizzling
1 brown onion, finely chopped
4 garlic cloves, thinly sliced, plus 4 more cut in half to rub on the bread
½ teaspoon chilli flakes
handful flat-leaf parsley, finely chopped
400 g (14 oz) tinned cannellini beans, drained
½ bunch kale, tough spines removed, chopped
400 g (14 oz) tinned crushed tomatoes
2 tablespoons chicken-style stock powder
parmesan rind
8 slices sourdough bread
½ cup (50 g) finely grated parmesan

OPTIONAL INGREDIENTS
more an optional action – reserve that aquafaba (the liquid from the cannellini beans) for your vegan mates

This soup relies on stale bread and a few tins of stuff from the pantry plus, of course, that most irritating of all vegetables to store: kale. However, you can switch this out for anything robust and leafy – even cabbage if you like.

This one is a chunky hot salad, let's be honest.

Heat the olive oil in a large heavy-based saucepan over medium heat. Add the onion and cook for 2 minutes, then add the sliced garlic, chilli flakes and parsley. Sauté, stirring, for 2–3 minutes.

Add the cannellini beans, kale and crushed tomatoes, stir, then reduce the heat to low.

Pour in 3 cups (750 ml) of water and stir in the stock powder. (I absolutely always wing this amount – especially as the salt level in stock powders can vary greatly, so follow the packet directions or do as I do: and don't!)

Next up is the magic umami step: throw in the parmesan rind then simmer for 20 minutes with the lid ajar.

Meanwhile, toast the sourdough. As soon as it pops, rub each slice with a chunk of cut garlic and sprinkle with parmy.

Add a piece of toast to the bottom of each serving bowl and cover with soup.

Drizzle with olive oil and serve with all the remaining toast.

Serves 4

2 eggplants (aubergines)
1 tablespoon extra virgin olive oil
2 teaspoons sea salt flakes
2 cups (370 g) steamed white rice

MAPO SAUCE
½ cup (125 ml) peanut oil
1½ tablespoons szechuan
   peppercorns
3 tablespoons finely grated
   fresh ginger
3 tablespoons grated garlic

1 bird's eye chilli, thinly sliced*
600 g (1 lb 5 oz) semi-firm tofu,
   crumbled
1 tablespoon shaoxing rice wine
2½ tablespoons toban djan
   (spicy bean sauce)
1½ tablespoons dark soy sauce
1 tablespoon crispy chilli oil
1 dried Chinese mushroom,
   ground to a powder
2 tablespoons soft brown sugar

2 teaspoons cornflour
   (cornstarch) mixed to a paste
   with 1 tablespoon cold water
⅔ cup (170 ml) chicken-style
   stock

OPTIONAL INGREDIENTS
finely chopped spring onions
   (scallions)

This comfort food is so lip-zingy you'll feel completely bee-stung. Spicy szechuan sticky sauce – usually seen carrying pork mince – becomes the slip and slide for tofu, which is piled high onto charred, chewy roast eggplant.

This one falls squarely into the 'I can't hear you hate on eggplant or tofu' basket. If you don't want this purely because of the concept, then you may skip forward.

Preheat the oven to 200°C (400°F) fan-forced.

Cut the eggplants in half lengthways. Use a knife to create a 1 cm (½ inch) wide crosshatch pattern on the eggplants' faces – make sure to keep the skin intact to act as a seal for liquids and juices.

Oil and salt** the eggplants and place them face down on a non-stick baking tray. Bake for 15 minutes.

Meanwhile, make the mapo sauce. Heat the peanut oil in a large, deep frying pan over medium heat, add the szechuan peppercorns, ginger,

garlic and bird's eye chilli and stir. Everything should soften and smell intensely after 3 minutes.

Add in the tofu and cook until just beginning to brown, around 5 minutes. Be careful not to over-stir, especially if the tofu is soft, or it will take on a jelly consistency.

Turn the heat up and pour in the shaoxing rice wine, stirring to deglaze the pan for around 3 minutes.

Stir in 2 tablespoons of toban djan, 2 teaspoons of dark soy sauce, the crispy chilli oil, the dried mushroom and 1 tablespoon of the brown sugar and combine well.

Add the cornflour paste and stock to the pan and lower the heat. Stir gently and allow the sauce to thicken, around 5 minutes.

In a small bowl, combine the remaining 2 teaspoons of toban djan, the remaining 1 tablespoon dark soy sauce and the remaining 1 tablespoon brown sugar and mix well.

When the eggplants are done, flip them onto their backs and brush them with this mixture. Turn the

oven to the grill setting and return the eggplant to the oven to crisp for a further 5 minutes.

Serve on steamed rice with a big scoop of zinging mapo sauce ladled on top and lots of spring onions (optional).

---

* The addition of bird's eye chilli takes this dish from sweet hum to holy mofo. It's a decision you need to make for yourself, plus chillies can be so unpredictably hot or not – so maybe toss a coin to decide.

** The salt is for flavour, not to reduce bitterness. Bitterness has been conveniently bred out of eggplant, so trust me, you don't need to extract it.

Serves 4

Mapo
Eggplant

Clearly not a soup, but
classic wet-bowl territory.

Minute Noodles

Noods should be the initiation into any cult. How you do it is up to you.
Thick and creamy, thin and soft, fat and slippery.

Serves 2, because you can really get into trouble if you share noods with more.

Spicy satay

1 tablespoon red curry paste
½ cup (125 ml) coconut cream
2 tablespoons peanut butter
4 cups (1 litre) chicken-style stock
½ lime
2 x 75 g (2½ oz) packets
    of 2-minute noodles
300 g (10½ oz) tinned corn,
    drained, or 1 corn cob,
    kernels only

1 bok choy, julienned
6-minute boiled egg, peeled
    and cut in half lengthways
chilli oil, for topping

Sauté the red curry paste in a
heavy-based saucepan over
medium heat until fragrant,
1–2 minutes. Add the coconut
cream and peanut butter and
whisk until smooth.

Add the stock and the juice from
the lime. Simmer for 2 minutes.

Add the noodles and corn kernels
and simmer for 2 minutes more.

Place the bok choy into two bowls
and ladle the soup/noodles over
each to blanch. Top with half an
egg each and some chilli oil.

Grate soup

1 tablespoon extra virgin olive oil,
   plus extra for drizzling
1 brown onion, grated
1 carrot, grated
1 celery stalk, grated
3 garlic cloves, grated
1 potato, grated
1 tomato, grated
1 zucchini (courgette), grated
4 cups (1 litre) vegetable stock
50 g (¾ oz) angel hair
   pasta, broken into
   4 cm (1½ inch) pieces
¼ cup (5 g) chopped
   flat-leaf parsley
fine salt and freshly ground
   black pepper, to taste

Heat the olive oil in a heavy-based saucepan over medium heat and sauté the onion, carrot, celery and garlic for 2 minutes.

Add the remaining veg and cook for a further 2 minutes.

Add the stock and bring to the boil. Reduce the heat and simmer for 5 minutes, or until the veg has softened.

Add the pasta and cook for a further 2 minutes. Stir through the parsley, season well and drizzle with extra virgin olive oil.

Golden pho

200 g (7 oz) dry rice noodles
4 cups (1 litre) beef-style stock
1 cm (½ inch) knob of ginger,
   peeled and grated
½ teaspoon turmeric powder
¼ teaspoon cinnamon
3 star anise
½ white onion, thinly sliced
¼ cup (7 g) Thai basil leaves
½ cup (10 g) Vietnamese
   mint leaves
½ cup (15 g) coriander
   (cilantro) leaves
2 lemon wedges

Pour boiling water over the rice noodles and let them soften. Set aside.

Bring the stock, ginger, turmeric, cinnamon, star anise and half the sliced white onion to the boil in a saucepan over medium–high heat.

Use tongs to place the noodles into two bowls. Top with the remaining sliced onion and pour the steaming broth on top. Add the herbs and a wedge of lemon.

This is the loaded chapter. The place where we shove a handful of delicious stuff in a carb. From fluffy buns and crispy grated spuds, to flavour pastes folded into pastry and lovely things squashed into dough.

This is the place to turn to when you need more than just a weeny leaf or two. This is the bopper where all the big girls play.

This isn't carb loading; it's loading a carb.

Carbs-filled-with-things Thursdays

Full Metal Jackets

But make them peaceful.

6 large brushed potatoes
butter and extra virgin olive oil,
  to serve

CURD DRESSING
⅔ cup (150 g) goat's curd
½ cup (125 g) sour cream
½ teaspoon finely snipped chives
½ teaspoon finely chopped dill
½ teaspoon finely grated
  lemon zest
¼ teaspoon garlic powder

SALSA
⅓ cup (60 g) pitted kalamata
  olives, finely chopped
1 cup (200 g) chopped tomatoes,
  seeds removed from large ones
¼ red onion, finely diced
2 Lebanese (short) cucumbers,
  seeds removed,* finely diced
¼ cup (60 ml) extra virgin olive oil
1 tablespoon white vinegar
1 teaspoon sea salt flakes
1 teaspoon dried oregano

OPTIONAL INGREDIENTS
chilli seems unnecessarily
aggressive but go for it

Start strong with the power of a jacket potato wrapped in foil, but with all the peace and love of a hippy child.

Disco jewels made with Greek salad ingredients straight from the Mediterranean blue zone confirm that this dish will help you live forever – I recommend fact-checking this, but it feels right to promote this recipe as the fountain of youth.

Preheat the oven to 230°C (450°F) fan-forced.

Wash and scrub the potatoes and pat dry. Wrap each spud in foil and place them on a baking tray. Bake for 1 hour 10 minutes.

Meanwhile, using hand-held electric beaters, beat the goat's curd and sour cream on medium speed until smooth and fluffy, around 2 minutes. Add the chives, dill, lemon zest and garlic powder and beat on high for 2 minutes. This dressing can be made ahead and stored in the fridge for 2 days in an airtight container.

To make the salsa, combine the olives, tomato, red onion and

cucumber in a small bowl and dress with the olive oil and white vinegar. Season with salt and dried oregano.

Once the potatoes are cooked and soft to the squeeze from a pair of tongs, remove the foil and place them on a serving platter.

Slice the potatoes lengthways, but not all the way through. Give them a gentle squeeze to push the flesh upwards towards the opening.

Top each potato with a big swipe of butter and then a dollop of curd dressing and splash the salsa all about. Drizzle with extra virgin olive oil and serve as is.

---

* Try as I might, I can never smoothly scrape cucumber seeds out of the centre. Maybe I need to get my spoons sharpened. I just cut a 5 mm (¼ inch) thick slice off one side of the cucumber, lay it flat and do the same on each side, rotating it until the flesh is trimmed and the seeds remain. Throw the seeds into a carafe of water for ultimate hydration – yes, we are now advancing into true health care.

Serves 6

Kimchi Rice Cakes

Okonomiyaki translates to
'what you want' and 'grilled',
which could really be the name
of so many things in my life.

RICE CAKES
1½ cups (275 g) cooked rice (whatever type you like)
½ cup (80 g) kimchi, finely diced
2 cups (150 g) shredded cabbage – I used wombok but you can use green
½ cup (50 g) grated cheddar
2 eggs
1 spring onion (scallion), white and green parts, finely diced
1 teaspoon sea salt flakes
2 teaspoons finely grated lime zest
rice bran oil spray
1½ tablespoons sesame seeds

OKONOMIYAKI SAUCE
2 tablespoons tomato sauce (ketchup)
1 tablespoon dark soy sauce
1 tablespoon maple syrup

TOPPINGS
kewpie mayo, for drizzling
finely shredded nori
pickled ginger
snipped chives

OPTIONAL INGREDIENTS
you can add 'what you want' to this – that's the point

These are ridiculously cute traditional Japanese pancakes.

They're also one of the funniest things I've ever made in a waffle machine.

You can mash in almost any veg or protein (hurray for leftovers!) for these pancakes, but here I've switched out flour for rice – which for some will be pleasing due to the lack of gluten. (Although considering the places you actually find gluten these days, don't assume the rest of the pancake is gluten free.)

In a large bowl, mix together the rice, kimchi, cabbage, cheddar, eggs, spring onion, salt and lime until well combined.

There are two ways to go here. Either spray a frying pan lightly with rice bran oil and heat over medium–high heat, or heat a sandwich press or waffle machine until hot and then spray it lightly with rice bran oil. If you do this in a sandwich press or waffle machine, you will get double-sided cooking, meaning it will cook a lot faster – but both techniques will work.

Using a ¼ cup (60 ml) measure, scoop the mixture onto the hotplate or into the pan. Sprinkle the top with a few sesame seeds. Lower the lid if using a machine (if you want your cake to be slightly thicker, don't press down too hard with the lid of the sandwich press).

Cook for approximately 5 minutes – or 5 minutes each side if using a frying pan – until golden brown and beginning to crisp.

As the cakes are cooking, make the sauce by mixing together the tomato sauce, dark soy sauce and maple syrup.

Place the cooked cakes onto a tray lined with baking paper and keep warm until serving.

To create a classic okonomiyaki pattern, squeeze mayonnaise and okonomiyaki sauce in alternating lines, then use a toothpick to swipe through the contrasting colours first one way, and then the other, creating a zigzag pattern.

Serve the pancakes with extra mayo and okonomiyaki sauce, nori, pickled ginger and chives.

Makes around 14 cakes

- 2 sheets (400 g) ready-made frozen shortcrust pastry
- 2 sheets (400 g) ready-made frozen puff pastry
- 2 tablespoons Bready Pesto from page 216, but without the breadcrumbs
- 6 slices grilled, marinated sweet potato*
- 1 cup (45 g) firmly packed baby spinach leaves
- 160 g (5¾ oz) provolone, thinly sliced

- 3 slices grilled, marinated eggplant (aubergine)*
- 2 tablespoons basil pesto (store-bought is fine)
- 125 g (4½ oz) buffalo mozzarella, thinly sliced
- 3 marinated artichokes, coarsely chopped*
- 1 tablespoon fresh oregano leaves
- 2 whole grilled, marinated capsicums (peppers), cut open at the edges to flatten*

- 8 slices grilled, marinated zucchini (courgette)*
- 1 tablespoon olive tapenade
- 2 teaspoons dijon mustard
- 1 egg, lightly beaten with 1 tablespoon of water

OPTIONAL INGREDIENTS
there's no garnish, this one already has everything

This pie has ALL the things: two pestos, a tapenade, grilled veg, two cheeses – all baked into the glory of golden flaky pastry. Sold? Same.

Preheat the oven to 200°C (400°F) fan-forced. Line a round pizza tray with baking paper.

Here's where I repeat things I saw on TikTok – I hope I explain it properly! This is how to turn two square pastry sheets into one giant round.

Roll each pastry sheet into a long cigar. Then roll the two cigars of shortcrust pastry into a large snail spiral. You can then use a rolling pin to roll this out into a 33 cm (13 inch) round. Place this on the pizza tray.

Repeat the process with the puff pastry sheets, and set aside to use as the lid when ready.

Layer the ingredients onto the shortcrust base one at a time, separating wet with cheese and salad. This is how I stacked from BOTTOM to TOP, leaving a 4 cm (1½ inch) edge: bready pesto + sweet potato + half the baby

spinach + a third of the provolone + eggplant + basil pesto + buffalo mozzarella + artichokes + fresh oregano + capsicum + remaining baby spinach + another third of the provolone + zucchini + tapenade + the remaining provolone.

Spread dijon on the underside of the pie lid.

Brush the edge of the pie base with the egg wash, reserving some for the top.

Cover the pie with the puff pastry lid and gently push out any air bubbles.

Trim the pastry so you are dealing with a neat-ish edge, then pinch and crimp the pastry the whole way around. Brush the top with the remaining egg wash.

TikTok trick #2. Rather than score the puff pastry, we are trussing it!

Tie cooking string underneath the pizza tray and up over the pie firmly. Repeat this another two to four times, depending on what size you would like to mark your pie slices at (3 strings = 6 slices).

Place in the oven and bake for 30 minutes, until puffed and golden brown.

Remove the string and allow the pie to cool slightly before cutting and serving.

---

* If you can't find these at a deli counter, then simply slice the raw veg into 5–7 mm (2–2¾ inch) thick slices. Roast in a preheated 200°C (400°F) fan-forced oven on a baking tray lined with baking paper for 20 minutes. Season well and set aside to cool. Drizzle with oil and red wine vinegar. The veg will keep for a week stored in an airtight container in the fridge.

Serves 6

Muffuletta Pie

The stacked pie that's
too good to be true.

Alfredo 'Shroom Soufra

If this is bad fashun then
I'm OK with that.

DUXELLES*

350 g (12 oz) mixed fresh
  mushrooms, coarsely chopped
¼ cup (30 g) shallots, thinly sliced
2 garlic cloves, finely chopped
1 tablespoon thyme leaves
⅓ cup (80 ml) vermouth or dry
  white wine
1 teaspoon fine salt
1½ tablespoons single (pure) cream

SOUFRA

1 x 375 g (13 oz) box filo pastry
  (18 sheets; the type kept in the
  fridge, not the freezer)

¼ cup (60 g) salted butter, melted
1 cup (250 ml) single (pure) cream
5 eggs
1 cup (250 ml) milk
1 cup (100 g) finely grated
  parmesan, plus extra
  for sprinkling
1 tablespoon each of finely
  snipped chives and finely
  chopped flat-leaf parsley leaves

OPTIONAL INGREDIENTS

salad

I'm not actually sure when the 90s called and demanded to be part of this book, but they certainly did and got waaay past security. In those days, cream and carbs were abundant, and the rich regret that follows eight mouthfuls of fettuccine alfredo was always forgotten when you were handed a menu.

A soufra is a very new experience for me, and I appreciate that this adaptation may not be doing the original as much justice as it should. But if I can somehow consume steamed pastry along with some crispy flaky bits and a rich custard of eggs, cream and milk, plus some madly aromatic fungi, then you have me, regrets and all.

Combine the mushrooms, shallots, garlic, thyme and vermouth in a frying pan over medium heat and cover for 15 minutes to wet fry. Remove the lid and continue to cook for 10 minutes, or until the mushrooms are soft and the liquid has evaporated.

Let the mushroom mixture cool before placing into a food processor with the salt and blending until finely chopped. Add the cream and blend until smooth.

When you are ready to assemble, make sure your filo pastry and mushroom mixture is at room temperature. Preheat the oven to 180°C (350°F) fan-forced. Lightly grease a shallow 20 x 31 cm (8 x 12½ inch) ovenproof dish – no deeper than 3 cm (1¼ inches).

This is the tricky bit – take a good look at the little photo there, it will help you. Lay one sheet of filo pastry on top of some baking paper.** Spread/brush some of the duxelles on the sheet. Place a second layer of filo pastry on top. Beginning at the short end of the pastry, gather the ends in a scrunching concertina*** fashion until it is a tight rectangular parcel. Place this closed concertina of pastry into the dish, snuggled up against one end. Repeat this process, tucking the scrunched pastry parcels into the dish as you go, until you have used all of the sheets of pastry. Adjust the parcels in the pan so they are evenly placed by spreading apart or pushing together as necessary.

Brush the top of the pastry with lots of lovely melted butter.

Bake for 15 minutes, or until the pastry is beginning to turn golden.

Meanwhile, whisk together the cream, eggs, milk and parmesan in a bowl.

Remove the dish from the oven and slowly pour the cream mixture into and around the crevices of the pastry. Allow time for the mixture to settle in place before adding more and filling up every little spot. Place the dish back in the oven for 20 minutes, or until just set.

Sprinkle generously with chives, parsley and extra parmesan.

Serve while still warm with a fresh salad.

---

* Duxelles is to puréed mushies as passata is to puréed toms … the fancy word.

** Keep the remaining filo pastry moist by covering with a slightly damp cloth.

*** The concertina scrunching does not need to be perfect.

Serves 6 with a salad

Scrap Burgers

Ultimate burger test: does juice run
down to your elbow? <tick>

400 g (14 oz) tinned chickpeas including the liquid (aquafaba)
1 teaspoon garlic powder
1 teaspoon onion powder
1 tablespoon dried oregano
1 tablespoon finely chopped flat-leaf parsley leaves
2 teaspoons beef-style stock powder
1 teaspoon paprika
200 g (7 oz) broccoli
1–2 beetroot, peeled
2 carrots

225 g (8 oz) halloumi, grated
¼ cup (35 g) plain (all-purpose) flour
4 tablespoons panko breadcrumbs
canola oil, for frying

OPTIONAL INGREDIENTS
toasted bread rolls, sliced cheese, mustard, shredded lettuce, pickles, sliced tomato, charred onions, BBQ/tom sauce

Shut the front door – no, no seriously. You'll need to fire up the BBQ for this baby and you don't want the couch to smell funny.

But also – Shut. The. Front. Door! This is one nasty (in a good way) VEGAN patty.

Plus, it uses up all the kids in the crisper who were never asked to dance this week. And as our 'hero before Thor' would say, 'Nobody puts baby in the corner.'

Yes, you can change the veg – you just need about 500–550 g (1 lb 3 oz) of hearty discard. Think cauli, 'shrooms, parsnip, beans, sweet potato … etc.

In a food processor, blend the chickpeas – liquid and all – with the garlic and onion powders, oregano, parsley, stock powder and paprika until chunky/smooth. Place into a large mixing bowl.

Chop the vegetables into manageable pieces of about 3–4 cm (1¼–1½ inches) and place in a food processor, a few cups at a time, to blitz until they are chopped quite fine.

Add the blitzed veg to the chickpea mix along with the grated halloumi, flour and panko crumbs and stir well to combine. The mix should resemble a mushy, thick paste, one you can form into patties of about ⅓ cup each.

Cook on an oiled preheated BBQ flat grill plate or in an oiled frying pan for about 5 minutes on each side. The burgers will become crisp and brown. Be careful as you flip to ensure they don't break up.

Enjoy them as you would a burger, rissole, meatball – do as you wish. It's nearly Friday after all.

Makes 8 patties

1½ cups (295 g) dried chickpeas (you can't use tinned here because they are too mushy)
1½ cups (295 g) split fava beans
2 cups (520 g) Greek-style yoghurt
1 carrot, coarsely chopped
1 celery stalk, roughly chopped
1 brown onion, coarsely chopped
2 beetroot, quartered with skins on

2 garlic cloves, smashed
1 teaspoon ground coriander
1 tablespoon ground cumin
2 tablespoons sea salt flakes
vegetable oil, for shallow frying
pita pockets
½ cup (80 g) cornichons or pickles, sliced or chopped
1 small salad onion, thinly sliced

PARSLEY SALAD
1 cup (20 g) flat-leaf parsley, leaves only
1 teaspoon sumac
1 teaspoon sea salt flakes
1 tablespoon extra virgin olive oil
2 tablespoons red wine vinegar

OPTIONAL INGREDIENTS
chilli sauce

This is a recipe that gives twice. Do the dirty work now and give your future self a night off when you can rip these falafels straight from the freezer into the pan.

OK, let's get all that overnight palaver done.

Place the chickpeas and fava beans in a large bowl and fill with water. Cover with a plate to stop cats/gnats bathing in it and leave overnight. The pulses will double in size.

Then we need to reverse the concept for the labne. Place a small strainer* over a bowl and line with three sheets of paper towel or, if you have it, muslin.

Pop the yoghurt in and allow it to drain/dry out overnight. The result is a rich sour cream cheese that can be balled up and stored in oil or rolled in herbs. The longer it drains, the thicker it will get. Please note: the draining contraption has to fit in the fridge so make sure it does before you use a sieve with a 40-foot handle.

The next step is super simple, but you need a food processor.

Blend the carrot, celery, brown onion and beets until finely diced. Add the drained pulses and blend until the mixture is grainy. Blend in the garlic, spices and salt.

Test a falafel by seeing if you can mush a small lump into a patty. It will stain your hands pink – more glamorous than turmeric. Maybe use spoons. If it holds together, then you can begin frying. If it doesn't, blend a bit more until it does.

Heat vegetable oil in a heavy-based frying pan over medium heat and shallow fry the falafels in batches, turning each falafel once as you cook. They should take about 5 minutes each.

Fry enough for your dinner and store any uncooked falafels in an airtight container in the freezer for up to 3 months.

For the salad, toss the parsley with the sumac, salt, olive oil and vinegar.

Serve the falafels warm on fresh pita with labne, parsley salad, pickles and salad onion.

* A shout out to those 500 g (1 lb 2 oz) ricotta baskets here – not only do they drain labne, but they also hold Lego mid-construction, collect toys from the bath in a single scoop, and are great little vessels to pick and rinse herbs in!

Serves 6 (and the same again in the freezer)

Beet
Falafel

Alert: you need to
start this one the day
before, but future you
will kiss you for it.

Giant Stuffed Rosti

It should look like you might feel
after a dusty day spent sunbaking –
golden, crispy, greasy and maybe
just a little gooey.

1.5 kg (3 lb 5 oz) potatoes,
  peeled and grated
1 brown onion, peeled and grated
2 teaspoons fine salt
½ cup (70 g) plain
  (all-purpose) flour
3 tablespoons extra virgin olive oil
2 garlic cloves, grated
2 zucchini (courgettes), grated
2 cups (250 g) grated mozzarella
1 cup (100 g) grated gruyere
1 teaspoon chilli flakes

1 tablespoon fresh
  oregano leaves
1 tablespoon lemon zest
2½ tablespoons salted butter
3 tablespoons polenta

OPTIONAL INGREDIENTS
chutney, but only to slow
you down

Do I think this is fun to make? Yes!

Is it fun to simply think about? 100% YES!

Will it make you more friends and increase attractiveness? Without question.

Stop mucking about and get serious about life with this giant stuffed rosti.

I don't know how to get you out of all that grating aside from suggesting that you buy an appliance that has a grating attachment – you won't look back; I promise you'll grate everything.

In a large bowl combine the potatoes, onion and salt. Set aside for 20 minutes, then squeeze out all of the excess moisture. Stir in the flour.

Heat 1 tablespoon of the olive oil in a large ovenproof non-stick pan over medium heat and cook the garlic until golden, about 2 minutes. Remove the garlic and wipe out the pan.

In a separate bowl, mix the zucchini, cheeses, chilli flakes, oregano, lemon zest and fried garlic.

Preheat the oven to 200°C (400°F) fan-forced.

Return the pan to medium–high heat and add the butter and remaining 2 tablespoons of olive oil. Once the butter is melted and bubbling, sprinkle in 1 tablespoon of polenta.

Place just over half the potato mixture into the pan, being careful not to displace the polenta. The best way to do this is to add little spoonfuls rather than a big splodge, and use a spatula to pat it down into a flat cake.

Distribute the zucchini mixture over the potato, leaving a 1 cm (½ inch) border. Top with the remaining potato mixture and pat it down. Sprinkle the remaining polenta on top and cook for around 10 minutes.

Place a large plate on top of the frying pan and hold the pan with a tea towel. Now flip the pan upside down so the rosti falls out onto the plate. Then very professionally slide the rosti back into the pan and fry for a further 10 minutes.

Now, place the pan in the oven for 20 minutes. The rosti will be golden, crispy and greasy when done … and maybe a little gooey if any cheese has escaped.

Allow the rosti to rest for 10 minutes and then flip it out onto a serving platter before cutting into sections.

I realise this recipe calls for a lot of flipping, but once you've done it once you won't look back. And who doesn't love a mad kitchen flip. Enjoy.

Disclaimer: Author does not recommend sunbaking until golden and crispy!

Serves 8 at brunch or as a side

Cuban Arancini

Left-over carbs + canned
corn + condiments.

4 cups (740 g) cooked white rice
125 g (4½ oz) tinned
   creamed corn
300 g (10½ oz) tinned corn
   kernels, drained
2 spring onions (scallions), white
   and green parts, finely sliced
2 eggs
½ cup (120 g) kewpie mayo
½ cup (50 g) grated parmesan
¼ cup (40 g) finely diced
   dill pickles
¼ cup (40 g) finely diced
   pickled jalapeños

1 garlic clove, crushed
250 g (9 oz) sliced mozzarella
   (16 slices)
2½ cups (150 g) panko
   breadcrumbs
olive oil spray
2 cups (500 ml) store-bought ajvar
   (red capsicum and eggplant
   sauce) or your favourite salsa

OPTIONAL INGREDIENTS
coriander, lime and extra chilli

Arancini is usually made with left-over risotto rice, but I don't often make risotto and if I do there's usually not much left over. But left-over steamed rice I often have in abundance, plus it's easy to add an extra container to a takeaway order – a great idea anyway to stash in the freezer for last-minute fry-ups.

All these flavours come together from a memory bank I have of eating Cuban sandwiches and grilled corn in NY. It's a great dinner, and even better with a frozen margarita.

Preheat the oven to 200°C (400°F) fan-forced.

Line a large baking tray with baking paper.

Blend ¼ cup (45 g) of the rice and all the creamed corn together on high speed in a food processor.

In a large bowl, combine this mixture with all the remaining ingredients except for the mozzarella, panko, oil and ajvar.

Using your hands to massage the ingredients together is both a satisfying and thorough way to mix everything well.

Set the mixture aside for 15 minutes so it can rest and the cooked rice can absorb some moisture.

Use a ¼ cup measure to portion out the rice mixture into 16 patties.

Place a slice of cheese into the centre of each patty and mould the rice around it.

Roll each patty in panko crumbs and spray lightly on both sides with the olive oil spray.

Place on the prepared tray and bake in the oven for 20 minutes, until golden and crisp.

Serve with a big dollop of ajvar or your favourite store-bought salsa.

Serves 4

4 cups (1 litre) vegetable oil
  for deep frying
2 cups (300 g) plain
  (all-purpose) flour
3 cups (750 ml) cold soda water
1 cauliflower, cut into marble-
  sized florets, washed and dried
6 crusty bread rolls
3 tablespoons softened
  salted butter
200 g (7 oz) cheddar, sliced
  or grated

1 baby cos lettuce, leaves
  separated and washed
½ cup (120 g) mayonnaise

PERI-PERI
6 bird's eye chillies
1 cup (270 g) grilled marinated
  capsicum (pepper), chopped
2 lemongrass stems, white parts
  only, chopped
¼ cup (7 g) chopped flat-leaf
  parsley, stems and all
¼ cup (7 g) chopped coriander
  (cilantro), stems and all

5 garlic cloves, chopped
¼ cup (60 ml) red wine vinegar
1 cup (250 ml) extra virgin olive oil
1 tablespoon sea salt flakes

SEASONING
2 teaspoons garlic powder
2 teaspoons paprika
1 teaspoon fine salt

OPTIONAL INGREDIENTS
a wire spider (I highly
recommend – you'll be amazed
how often you use it)

**This isn't a traditional recipe.
I have made it from flavours
I've picked up – likely similar
to a winemaker with a bad nose
remaking something they
drank once.**

**The lemongrass comes from
left field but I wouldn't leave
it out now because I just love
the addition and I reckon you'll
like it too.**

**Also, if you want to make a
gateway sauce for kids, remove
the bird's eye and add it back in
slowly until they can handle it
over time.**

For the peri-peri, use a food
processor to blend everything
together until smooth.

Transfer to a small saucepan and
simmer over medium heat for
15–20 minutes. It shouldn't reduce;
however, you do want the fresh
things to cook off in the oil and
for the solids to separate from
the liquids, creating an iridescent
oily sauce.

Set aside until ready to use. You
can store this sauce in an airtight
container in the fridge for a week.

Combine the seasoning
ingredients in a small bowl
and set aside.

Depending on the size of the large
heavy-based saucepan you are
using, fill it only ⅓ –½ of the way up
with vegetable oil. Oil expands and
froths when you fry and spilling
can cause a fire. Just make sure
the oil is deep enough for a batch
of florets to swim in. Heat the oil
to 180–190°C (350–375°F).

Use a large mixing bowl to very
loosely combine the flour and the
soda. Lumps are fine and will give
you crispy fun bits.

Using a wire scoop, dunk a batch
of cauliflower into the batter and
then into the oil.

It should take about 2 minutes for
them to become golden and crisp.
Scoop cooked pieces out and
place them on a wire rack to drain.
Throw on the seasoning as you go.

Once you've made it through
the batch cooking, preheat the
oven grill.

Cut open the bread rolls, butter
liberally (yes, here we are again),

layer with cheese slices and grill
until bubbling, 1–2 minutes.

Fill with crispy lettuce, a swipe of
mayo, a huge drizzle of peri-peri
and a scoop of crunchy cauli.
Dribble on more sauce and mayo,
crunch it all together and chomp
on in.

I owe my 16-year-old beach body
to daily swims and these good
Portuguese Bondi burgers.

Serves 6

Peri-Peri
Popcorn Cauli

Once you start this whole ordeal,
there's no stopping or turning back.

Calzleme

Gozleme + Calzone
= Calzleme

DOUGH

2¼ cups (335 g) self-raising flour
1 cup (260 g) Greek-style yoghurt
1 teaspoon fine salt
1 teaspoon extra virgin olive oil,
  plus extra for oiling the bowl

FILLING

120 g (4¼ oz) thawed and
  squeezed spinach, from a
  250 g/9 oz packet of frozen
  spinach
3 marinated long-stem artichokes,
  chopped
1 small garlic clove, smashed

pinch of chilli flakes
2 teaspoons extra virgin olive oil,
  plus extra for brushing the
  calzleme
1 teaspoon white wine vinegar
fine salt and freshly ground black
  pepper, to taste
150 g (5½ oz) fresh ricotta
⅔ cup (100 g) feta
½ cup (65 g) grated mozzarella,
  plus ¼ cup (35 g) more to
  sprinkle on top of the spinach
1 lemon, zest finely grated, cut
  into wedges to serve

OPTIONAL INGREDIENTS

A BBQ; it must have a flat plate and
a lid. Grill on medium heat with the
lid closed for 10–15 minutes,
turning the calzleme once.

**This recipe is a piece-together of
a couple of favourites and sees
cheese and spinach – gozleme
standards – shaped like calzone.**

**But most importantly: what
do calzone and gozleme have
in common? My love. Oh, and
flatty dough.**

In the bowl of a standmixer fitted
with the dough hook, place 2 cups
(300 g) of the flour, the yoghurt
and salt and mix on medium speed
for 2–3 minutes. Add 1 teaspoon of
olive oil and keep mixing, adding
more flour if needed, 1 tablespoon
at a time, until a soft, elastic dough
forms. Shape the dough into a
ball and oil a large bowl. Place the
dough into the bowl, cover and
leave in a warm place to rest for
30 minutes.

Meanwhile, for the filling, combine
the spinach, artichokes, garlic,
chilli flakes, 2 teaspoons olive oil
and white wine vinegar in a bowl
and season.

In another bowl, combine the
ricotta, feta, ½ cup (65 g) of the
mozzarella and the lemon zest.

Preheat the oven to 200°C (400°F)
fan-forced. Line two baking trays
with baking paper.

Place the rested dough ball on
a piece of baking paper and cut
it into quarters.

Take one piece of dough and
dust it with the remaining ¼ cup
(35 g) of flour. Roll it out to around
15 x 25 cm (6 x 10 inches). You're
going to put filling ingredients on
one half of the dough, leaving the
other half bare. Spread a quarter
of the cheese mixture over half of
the dough, leaving a 1 cm (½ inch)
border. Top with a quarter of the
spinach mixture. Sprinkle a little of
the extra mozzarella on top of the
spinach then fold the dough over
the filled side. Press and pinch
to seal the edges, removing air
bubbles as you go.

Repeat with the remaining three
dough pieces and cheese and
spinach mixtures.

Brush both sides of the calzleme
with olive oil and place them on
the trays. Bake for 20 minutes,
swapping oven positions at

10 minutes to ensure they
cook evenly. The calzleme will be
golden brown, puffy and crisp
when ready.

Slice and serve with lemon
wedges.

Serves 4

Dumplings

Basically a nood's best friend, but cool enough to stand alone, these perfect little pockets of punchy flavour deserve their own sauce but, of course, sharing those is the best bit. The concept of eating dumplings has evolved from 'snack' to 'meal' because, like most tiny things, they are great – and one or two is never enough.

Serves 4

Steamed Vegetable
Dumplings

Fluffy Corn &
Tofu Dumplings

Steamed Vegetable Dumplings

125 g (4½ oz) mushrooms (any variety you like), finely diced
1 teaspoon finely grated ginger
2 spring onions (scallions), white and green parts, chopped
1 garlic clove, smashed
1 tablespoon peanut oil
fine salt and freshly ground black pepper, to taste
1 celery stalk, finely diced
1 bok choy, finely diced
½ cup (80 g) water chestnuts, chopped
½ cup (125 g) bamboo shoots, chopped
2 teaspoons mushroom oyster sauce
½ teaspoon sesame oil
2 teaspoons cornflour (cornstarch)
1 pack square wonton wrappers
1 carrot, sliced thinly on the diagonal
2 tablespoons soy sauce
1 teaspoon rice vinegar
1 teaspoon chilli oil
1 teaspoon sesame seeds, toasted

Over high heat in a large non-stick pan, sauté the mushrooms, ginger, spring onion and garlic for 5 minutes in peanut oil. Season well with S+P.

Add the celery, bok choy, water chestnuts, bamboo shoots, mushroom oyster sauce and sesame oil. Toss well to combine then remove the pan from the heat. This is not about cooking the veg, but tossing everything well and releasing some flavour with a little warmth. The veg also speeds up the cooling process.

Once cool, stir through the cornflour.

Place a teaspoon of mix in the centre of a wrapper, wet the edges with water and seal well by pressing together. Repeat with the remaining mix and wrappers.

Steam over boiling water, with each dumpling sitting on a carrot slice to prevent sticking, for around 20 minutes.

Combine the soy sauce, vinegar, chilli oil and sesame seeds to create a dipping sauce.

Makes 30

Fluffy Corn & Tofu Dumplings

300 g (10½ oz) firm tofu
125 g (4½ oz) tinned creamed corn
⅔ cup (135 g) tinned corn kernels, drained
2 tablespoons garlic chives, finely snipped
1 celery stalk, finely diced
1½ teaspoons fine salt
¼ teaspoon Chinese five-spice
1 teaspoon finely grated ginger
1 egg white, whisked until fluffy
1 tablespoon cornflour (cornstarch)
16 x 20 cm (8 inch) round rice paper sheets
⅓ cup (40 g) sesame seeds
145 ml (4¾ fl oz) peanut oil
3 spring onions (scallions), white and green parts, chopped
10 cm (4 inch) knob of ginger extra, peeled and grated
1 teaspoon sesame oil
2 tablespoons mushroom oyster sauce
2 tablespoons tahini

In a large mixing bowl break up the tofu with a whisk, then fold in the creamed corn, corn kernels, garlic chives, celery, 1 teaspoon of the salt, the Chinese five-spice and the 1 teaspoon grated ginger. Once combined, add the egg white and cornflour.

On a 30 x 40 cm (12 x 16 inch) tray lined with baking paper, smooth the mixture out into a rectangle around 1 cm (½ inch) thick. Place it into the freezer for 30 minutes. Remove from the freezer and cut it into 8 cm (3¼ inch) squares.

Soften one sheet of rice paper at a time (follow the packet directions) and place a square of mixture in the centre. Fold over the edges to enclose. Do a double layer of the wrapping, flipping the square over to seal the open side.

Sprinkle the sesame seeds onto a plate. Press the dumplings into the sesame seeds.

Fry the dumplings in 1 tablespoon of the peanut oil over medium heat, turning once, until crisp on both sides – around 4 minutes a side.

Place the spring onion, ginger and remaining ½ teaspoon of salt in a small bowl. Heat the remaining peanut oil and the sesame oil in a small pan, then pour it on top of the spring onion and ginger for a dipping sauce.

Combine the mushroom oyster sauce and tahini in a small bowl for a sweet sesame dipping sauce.

Makes 8

Crispy Eggplant Momos

½ brown onion, finely diced
3 tablespoons peanut oil
2 garlic cloves, smashed
1 eggplant (aubergine), cut
    into 1 cm (½ inch) cubes
½ teaspoon szechuan
    peppercorns
2 tablespoons rogan josh
    curry paste
1½ tablespoons black vinegar
1 teaspoon soft brown sugar
1 pack round gow gee wrappers
1 cup (260 g) Greek-style yoghurt
2 tablespoons achar pickles

Over high heat in a large non-stick frying pan, sauté the onion for 5 minutes in 2 tablespoons of the peanut oil. Add the garlic and eggplant and cook for a further 5 minutes. Reduce the heat to medium. Stir through the szechuan and curry paste and cook until fragrant and everything is softening, around 10 minutes.

Remove from the heat and add the vinegar and sugar. Stir well and allow to cool.

Place a teaspoon of the mixture in the centre of a wrapper, wet the edges and seal well by pressing together. Repeat with the remaining wrappers and mixture.

Place a single layer (8–10) of dumplings in a large non-stick frying pan with the remaining

1 tablespoon peanut oil on medium heat. Fry for 5 minutes, then add 1 cup (250 ml) of water and cover with a lid. Simmer for 10 minutes, or until the momos are cooked through and the liquid has been absorbed.

Serve on yoghurt and achar.

Makes 30

Crispy
Eggplant
Momos

Throw-it-together munchies that morph and grow depending on the number of guests (invited or not).

The criteria for this chapter are:
1. Use it up and 2. Make it irresistible.

There's a lot of 'using up' done on Friday at our house, when we seek out the forgotten ambitions that have been left in the veg drawer to flop. I don't particularly love hindsight – my response is to embrace what wasn't and turn it into what will be. Making it irresistible and easy entails fun flavours, silly ideas, lots of dipping, everything hand-held and, if all else fails, fry it.

Also, all of these recipes are designed to be shared snacks – halfway between carrot sticks and a roast dinner in terms of filling.

Phat Snack Fridays

Disco Fries

Vodka sodas might not make you
any friends, but this gravy will.

FRIES
1.8 kg (4 lb) potatoes, washed and
   cut into 1–1.5 cm (½ inch) sticks,
   skins on
¼ cup (60 ml) rice bran oil
110 g (3¾ oz) buffalo mozzarella,
   torn or sliced

GRAVY
120 g (4¼ oz) field mushrooms
2 tablespoons balsamic vinegar
¼ cup (60 ml) extra virgin olive oil
180 g (6 oz) carrots, cut into 3 cm
   (1¼ inch) chunks

2 brown onions, cut into
   3 cm (1¼ inch) chunks
3 celery stalks, cut into
   3 cm (1¼ inch) chunks
1 garlic head, cut in half
   horizontally, skin on
½ bunch thyme sprigs
2 tablespoons rosemary leaves
¼ cup (60 ml) red wine
1 tablespoon dijon mustard
1 tablespoon (2 g) dried porcini
   mushrooms, soaked in ¼ cup
   (60 ml) boiling water and
   allowed to cool

1 tablespoon salted butter
2 tablespoons plain
   (all-purpose) flour
2 cups (500 ml) beef-style stock
fine salt and freshly ground black
   pepper, to taste

OPTIONAL INGREDIENTS
midnight vodka sodas

**Aka poutine, which I don't love as
a word, but as with anything with
heritage, we should definitely
learn the truth, appreciate it and
accept it. However, 'Disco Fries'
sounds fun, and helps authorise
their consumption after hours.**

**I am not sure what kind of fries
and gravy dancer you are, but
for me – half crisp, half wet sog is
a delightful concept. I like gravy
levels to be high enough to warrant
the question, 'Is it … soup?'**

**My advice is to make this gravy,
freeze it and have it ready
because – vegetarian or not –
when you want chips and gravy
with a slap of mozzarella, you
don't want any delay.**

First up, soak the potatoes in
cold water for a few hours to
remove starch.

Preheat the oven to 200°C (400°F)
fan-forced.

For the gravy, tear the field
mushrooms into rough chunks
and throw them in a bowl
with the balsamic vinegar and
1 tablespoon of the olive oil.
Toss and set aside.

Toss the carrots, onions,
celery, garlic and herbs in the
remaining olive oil and place
in a large ovenproof frying pan
or flameproof baking dish with
¼ cup (60 ml) of water.

Roast for 15 minutes, then add
the marinated field mushrooms
and toss well. Roast for another
15 minutes until the veg are
golden and caramelised.

Remove the pan or dish from the
oven and place on the stove over
medium–high heat. Deglaze with
red wine to release all the sticky
good bits.

Increase the oven temperature
to 220°C (425°F). Dry the potatoes,
toss them in rice bran oil and
spread them out on a baking tray
or two. Season with a big pinch of
salt. Bake for 30 minutes, turning
once or twice, until golden brown.

Add the dijon mustard, the soaked
porcini (and the liquid) to the pan
on the stove, and stir until most
of the liquid is absorbed, around
10 minutes. Reduce the heat to
medium and add the butter and
flour, stirring constantly to form
a smooth paste.

Add the stock slowly, and
continue to stir until a smooth
gravy has formed, then remove
from the heat.

Mash the veg with a potato
masher, making sure to squish
out all the garlic from the head,
then strain the gravy into a bowl,
catching all the liquid. Push and
mash the veg through as much
as possible. For a really silky gravy
blend the strained liquid until very
smooth. Season to taste and keep
warm until ready to use.

Serve the chips loaded with gravy
and torn mozzarella.

Serves 4

Salt & Battery Floral

Zucchini flower season is short and
sweet, so change whatever cooking
plans you have when the blooms
appear and make this.

16 zucchini flowers (with the baby zukes attached if you're lucky)
4 cups (1 litre) rice bran or vegetable oil

STUFFING
230 g (8½ oz) fresh ricotta
1 garlic clove, smashed
1 teaspoon white miso paste
1 teaspoon finely grated fresh ginger
2 teaspoons mirin
2 teaspoons finely grated lemon zest
¼ cup (20 g) finely shredded nori

MAYO
½ cup (120 g) kewpie mayo
1 tablespoon wasabi
1 teaspoon lemon juice

BATTER
1¾ cups (260 g) plain (all-purpose) flour
1½ cups (375 ml) soda water
1 teaspoon fine salt

OPTIONAL INGREDIENTS
shichimi togarashi (Japanese chilli seasoning)

Yes, we know how to do Italian-style stuffed zucchini flowers – or it's easy enough to find out – but do you know how to do them Japanese-style?

I didn't, but I do now, and I just don't know how I can go back – knowing me I'll likely go back and forth forever. That's the beauty of food – tiny changes with ingredients and we have a whole new story to inspire us.

I went deep into method cooking and used long wooden chopsticks to manoeuvre the zuke flowers in and out of the batter and oil. The result was a pair of sticks with so many deep fried layers baubling at one end that they looked like spent matches. Did I chew the delicious crispy golden dagwood-ish dough off the ends? Great question. I'm not telling.

For the stuffing, combine the ricotta, garlic, miso, ginger, mirin, zest and nori in a bowl and stir until well mixed.

The next step, like icing a cake, is a bit fiddly. But unlike an iced cake, the end result is really satisfying. (This is all true unless you REALLY love cake more than fried salty stuff. Divisive statement I know.)

Gently peel open the petals and remove the stamens. You can leave them in, but more room for cheese sounds ideal to me. Spoon in the filling, pressing it in with the back of the spoon. Pros: suitable for laziness; cons: messy, rough.

Alternatively, use a piping bag or snap-lock bag with the corner cut off to pipe the stuffing in. Pros: neat; cons: an extra step as you look for bags.

Whichever you do, twirl the ends to close the filling in and move on. The filled flowers can sit on a baking tray lined with baking paper until you're ready to fry.

Prep the wasabi mayo by adding the ingredients to a bowl and doing a half mix. I like it unmixed, because you can swipe hard right or left and get different flavours. But again, don't be led by my enthusiasm – mix well if you like.

Now make the batter by combining the flour, soda water and salt in a bowl. Don't overmix this: it's not laziness, it's deliberate.

Do what I say here: you want soda bubbles and a few flour pockets to keep the batter light.

Heat the oil in a deep saucepan or wok* over medium–high heat to 190°C (375°F).

Dunk a flower into the batter, then lower it into the pan. It should bubble and begin to turn golden in 2 minutes. Gently turn it with a slotted spoon and cook for a further 2 minutes. Continue cooking in batches you can handle and allow the oil to reheat after a few goes.

Place the flowers on a wire rack to drain before serving.

---

* A wok is a great frying vessel because you can have the oil semi-deep but you still have room to scoop the contents out easily.

Serves 4–6 as a snack

3¼ cups (500 g) plain
(all-purpose) flour
1 teaspoon instant yeast
1 tablespoon fine salt
2 teaspoons white
(granulated) sugar
2 tablespoons extra virgin olive oil
1½ cups (375 ml) warm water
400 g (14 oz) tinned
crushed tomatoes
390 g (13¾ oz) tomato passata
(puréed tomatoes)

TAPENADE
½ cup (80 g) pitted
kalamata olives
½ cup (85 g) pitted Sicilian olives
2 garlic cloves, smashed
1 teaspoon dried oregano
3 tablespoons rosemary leaves,
chopped
2 teaspoons fine salt
½ cup (125 ml) extra virgin olive oil

OPTIONAL INGREDIENTS
some kind of bitter spritz

The whole finger pressing into wet squelchy oily dough thing on Instagram/TikTok is sexual – we know that, right? Yes, I'm into it … but alone. It seems like it should be done in private – like mud wrestling and opening your bank app.

Twice-baking this focaccia is inspired by my good mate Monty, the king of playful aperitivo.

Place the flour, yeast, salt and sugar in the bowl of a standmixer fitted with the dough hook and combine on medium speed. Make a deep well in the centre of the dry ingredients, then add the oil and warm water. Turn the mixer back on to medium and mix for 10–12 minutes, or until the dough is combined and stretchy.

Cover with plastic wrap and allow to prove somewhere warm for 1–1½ hours. Ideal spots: in a switched-off dryer that has just been on for 5 minutes, on a sunny kitchen bench where there is no draught or, if you are fancy enough, in a warming drawer.

My editor puts hers under the duvet in her bed with a hot water bottle. Good idea, although I would probably forget it was there until the shocking discovery later that evening.

Meanwhile, place a strainer over a bowl and line it with some paper towel. Tip the crushed toms in and set aside to drain while you wait.

To make the tapenade, combine all the ingredients in a small bowl and roughly blitz with a stick blender until it is a chunky paste. Set aside.

Once the dough has risen, punch it down and flop it out onto a lightly floured surface. Knead for 5 minutes, then stretch it out on the bench so you have a rectangle about 3 cm (1¼ inches) thick.

Spread the tapenade out over the dough, then fold the dough over onto itself. Fold the dough in half another six or so times (you are folding in the filling here). The chunky, uneven channels of filling make for a really delightful experience when eating this bread. So don't overwork it.

Lightly oil an ovenproof dish or – as I used – a cast-iron frying pan. Place the filled dough into the pan and push it out to the edges. Cover with plastic wrap and allow it to prove again for 30 minutes (it should double in size).

Preheat the oven to 230°C (450°F) fan-forced.

Combine the drained crushed toms with the passata in a bowl (use the drained tomato liquid for something else).

Spoon half of the tomato mixture over the risen dough.

Bake for 15 minutes, then add the remaining tomato mixture. Bake for another 15–20 minutes, until the top is deep red from the tomatoes and the dough is fluffy and spongy.

Allow it to cool, then slice it into crispy-edged fluffy bread strips and enjoy with all your fave snack mates.

Serves 8 as a snack

Deep-Pan
Aperitivo

This is an anti-finger-
sticking situation.

Buffalo Jals

Pronounced Hals.

600 g (1 lb 5 oz) jalapeños
1 cup (230 g) cream cheese
1 cup (100 g) grated
   smoked cheddar
1 garlic clove, smashed
1 tablespoon chives,
   finely snipped
½ teaspoon cayenne pepper
¼ cup (35 g) plain
   (all-purpose) flour
1 egg, lightly whisked with
   1 tablespoon water
1 cup (60 g) panko breadcrumbs

4 cups (1 litre) canola oil
   (or any high heat oil you prefer),
   for deep frying

BUFFALO SAUCE
2 tablespoons tomato
   sauce (ketchup)
⅓ cup (80 ml) hot sauce
   (I use Frank's RedHot)
1½ tablespoons tabasco
1 tablespoon soft brown sugar
¼ cup (60 g) cold salted butter,
   cubed

BLUE CHEESE DIP
75 g (2½ oz) soft blue cheese
2 tablespoons mayo
¼ cup (70 g) Greek-style yoghurt

OPTIONAL INGREDIENTS
margaritas seem more essential
than optional, but your call

Let's take something delicious, fresh and bright, stuff it with cheese, crumb it and fry it, shall we?

Yes, great idea.

But make it really spicy so we forget and rub our eyes while we work.

Ugh, OK.

No, no, you don't have to do the last bit – it just serves as a warning to either chuck on some dishwashing gloves OR wash your hands 'covid' intensely after you've finished.

The deep-frying scenario begins again. I have a hot tip: buy a camp stove and fry outside. 'Thank you', screams your wardrobe, couch and indoor air quality.

I often suggest a litre of oil but this depends on the pot you intend to fry in. Ideally, you want something deep and sort of wide. You should be able to add enough oil so that the thing you're frying can sink below the oil without hitting the base. But there should also be at least half of the pot edge above the oil so that it doesn't boil over.

Halve the jalapeños and remove the seeds. Keep the handy stalks attached.

Combine the cream cheese, cheddar, garlic and chives in a bowl, then divide the mixture in half. Spike one half with cayenne pepper – because roulette without real bullets is fun.

Use a teaspoon to smoosh the stuffing mix into the open faces of the jals.

Dip and toss each chilli into the flour, dunk them into the egg wash, then roll them straight into the panko crumbs. Set aside in the fridge until ready to cook.

For the sauce, heat the tomato sauce, hot sauce, tabasco and brown sugar in a saucepan over medium heat, stirring, until the sugar is dissolved. Whisk in the cold butter until the sauce is smooth and silky. This can be stored in the fridge.

For the dip, use a stick blender to blitz the blue cheese, mayo and yoghurt until mostly smooth (some chunks of blue are good) and store in the fridge until ready to use.

Heat the oil to medium-high heat (180–190°C/350–375°F), then lower the jals in to fry until golden brown, around 3 minutes all up, including turning. Carefully scoop them out with a slotted spoon or wire scoop so that the crumb coating isn't broken.

Place on a rack to drain.

Serves 6 as a snack

A Private Artichoke

It's distressing but also completely pleasing that no one in my household joins me in my obsession with this thistle.

artichokes, as many as you'd like

AIOLI
1 cup (235 g) mayonnaise
1 head garlic, cut in half
   horizontally, skin on, drizzled
   with oil, wrapped in foil and
   baked at 180°C (350°F)
   fan-forced for 30 minutes
1 tablespoon dijon mustard
1 tablespoon lemon juice
1 tablespoon finely snipped chives
   or flat-leaf parsley leaves

GARLIC BUTTER
¼ cup (60 g) salted butter
¼ cup (60 ml) extra virgin olive oil
3 garlic cloves, finely chopped

STUFFING
¼ cup (30 g) breadcrumbs
1 tablespoon extra virgin olive oil
1 tablespoon finely grated
   lemon zest
¼ cup (25 g) finely
   grated parmesan

1 garlic clove, smashed
1 tablespoon finely chopped
   flat-leaf parsley leaves
1 tablespoon dried oregano
1 tablespoon salted butter

OPTIONAL INGREDIENTS
everything and nothing

I've devoured artichokes since I was seven. The garlic butter, the oily crumb, the process of pulling the leaves, the final chomping on the heart, the sweetness of everything you taste afterwards. Pure joy.

As much as you want to share such a pleasure, if those around you don't get it then you must find peace with this. I only ever buy two artichokes. It's a gesture, but a gesture I can cover up and eat in its entirety if no one else wants to join me. Find yourself something they hate and love it alone.

The artichokes should be as green as possible. Avoid purple – this indicates the centre is turning to thistle and could probably kill you if consumed.

Also, the best eating of these is done by scraping your bottom teeth along the inner flesh of the petal. F*cking delicious.

These are my two favourite ways with artichokes. The butter dipping situation is midweek quick and messy; my immediate response to new season globes. The stuffed beauty takes a little

longer, but I file that under self-care (aka 'the rest of you mofos can make your own dinner').

To prepare the chokes for dipping, there's no need to trim them, unless you want to tidy them a bit.

Cook the artichokes in rapidly boiling water for 20 minutes, or until one of the tough outer leaves peels off easily with tongs. Remove them from the water and drain upside down in a bowl.

Mix the aioli ingredients together in a bowl until smooth. Store what you don't use (around 4 serves) in a jar in the fridge for a week.

For the garlic butter, melt the butter with the oil and garlic in a small saucepan over medium heat, stirring occasionally until it begins to bubble and the garlic turns golden, around 5 minutes. Remove from the heat and serve warm in a bowl.

Eat the chokes warm, dipping every petal into the sauces.

For the stuffed chokes, preheat the oven to 200°C (400°F) fan-forced. Line a baking tray with baking paper.

Cut the top 2 cm (¾ inch) off the artichokes and pry your way in to scoop out the centre, pulling back leaves as much as you can. Trim the stalk flush with the base of the artichoke so that it sits facing up.

Combine all the stuffing ingredients except the butter in a bowl and set aside.

Boil the artichokes as you did for dipping, then use a spoon to pack every leaf with as much stuffing as possible. Place on the baking tray, top with butter and bake for 15 minutes, or until golden.

Eat warm.

Serves 1, maybe 2

1 long green chilli
3 green tomatoes or kumatos
2 stems coriander (cilantro),
    stems and leaves separated,
    chopped
pinch of fine salt
1 avocado, peeled and
    stone removed
1 tablespoon pickled jalapeños
1 tablespoon pickle juice from
    the jalapeños
2 tablespoons extra virgin olive oil
2 tablespoons lime juice
1 spring onion (scallion),
    roughly chopped

1 green capsicum (pepper),
    finely diced
1 brown onion, finely diced
2 garlic cloves, smashed
1 teaspoon unsweetened
    cocoa powder
410 g (14½ oz) tinned young
    jackfruit, drained and broken up
1 tablespoon Mexican Seasoning
    from page 216
1 tablespoon finely grated
    lime zest
¼ cup (60 ml) vegetable stock
fine salt and freshly ground black
    pepper, to season

1 quantity Baby Beshy
    from page 215
2 cups (200 g) grated cheddar
1 tablespoon finely snipped chives
20 Asian pancakes (the type used
    for peking duck) or mini
    tortillas/soft tacos
2 cups (500 ml) vegetable oil
    for shallow frying

OPTIONAL INGREDIENTS
extra lime to squeeze on top,
and chilli sauce

Having grown up on a farm, it doesn't feel quite right to me to eat something processed before I've eaten the real thing. However, I haven't eaten fresh jackfruit. So, yes, I'm a hypocrite. In the past I've scoffed at jackfruit like a jerk.

BUT, while writing this book, although I didn't crave meat, I did crave new textures. Jackfruit is not a replacement for pulled pork – it's a stand-alone delicious, juicy, fibrous plant (think artichoke hearts!) that doesn't break down too much (looking at you, cauliflower) and is perfect for a ridiculously crispy fried taco with cheese sauce AND spicy avo dressing. Plus, the carnivores at home ate it without question.

Burn the green chilli skin over a naked stovetop flame, BBQ or under the grill. You are going for the charred skin flavour!

Using a food processor, blitz the tomatoes, green chilli, half of the chopped coriander stems and a pinch of salt until puréed. Set aside. In the same processor, blend the remaining coriander stems, avo, jalapeños, pickle juice, 1 tablespoon of the olive oil, 1 tablespoon of the lime juice and the spring onion until smooth. Set this aside also.

In a large, deep frying pan, sauté the capsicum and onion in the remaining olive oil over high heat for 5 minutes, or until starting to char slightly.

Turn the heat down to medium and add the garlic, cocoa, jackfruit and Mexican Seasoning. Sauté for another 2 minutes, then add the blended tomato sauce, remaining lime juice, zest and stock.

Reduce the heat to low, cover and simmer for 10 minutes, then season with salt and pepper. You can make this ahead and store it in the fridge overnight. Bring it to room temperature before frying.

Meanwhile, make the Baby Beshy, then add the cheese, whisking, until it's bubbling and smooth, around 5 minutes. Add the chives and remove from the heat. Keep warm until serving.

Place a couple of tablespoons of jackfruit mix in the centre of each duck pancake (or mini tortilla/soft

taco). Bring the sides together and secure with a toothpick to make them 'fry proof', weaving in and out across the top.

Heat the veg oil to 180–190°C (350–375°F) over medium heat in a high-sided frying pan. Pan-fry the filled tacos in batches, carefully turning so they cook for 1–2 minutes on each side. Remove when golden and place on a rack to drain.

Remove the toothpicks and serve scattered with the chopped coriander leaves, with the spicy avo dressing and cheese sauce alongside.

Makes 20

Fried Mini Tacos

I stand with tinned jackfruit.

S+P Tofu Cups

Would you like a crispy
cold beer with that?

500 g (1 lb 2 oz) semi-firm tofu
1 tablespoon fine salt
¼ teaspoon Chinese five-spice
2 spring onions (scallions), white
    parts sliced into 7 cm (2¾ inch)
    julienne, green tops thinly sliced
    into rings
1 cos lettuce
1 Lebanese (short) cucumber,
    cut into 7 cm (2¾ inch) batons
¼ cup (60 ml) hoisin sauce
1 lemon, cut into wedges

¼ cup (30 g) cornflour
    (cornstarch)
2 cups (500 ml) vegetable oil
2 rice paper rounds (the dry
    ones used for rolls), broken
    into eighths

OPTIONAL INGREDIENTS
Chilli Crisp from page 215

The hot oil smell in this recipe triggers me, taking me back to a time when I was forced to say, 'Would you like fries with that?' 183 times a day. But honestly, all this crispy biz is full of fresh veg, and has actual produce crunch, not just fried crunch ... so if we think about it, it's basically a green smoothie.

Now, for the tofu, have a little foresight (the kind and calm sister to hindsight, who is irritating and mildly patronising). Remove the tofu from its watery pack and place it on a tray lined with a wad of paper towel. Place another wad on top and top that with another tray with a bit of weight on it – no more than 400 g. Set aside for 2–3 hours (you could do this in the morning before work and chuck it in the fridge!). This just helps the airy brick release all the liquid it carries.

OK, let's sort our mise en place.

In a small bowl, combine the salt and Chinese five-spice so it's ready to sprinkle. Place the green spring onion rounds in another dish.

Arrange the washed lettuce, julienned spring onion and cucumber on a platter (or in separate bowls).

Put the hoisin into a reasonably easy vessel to dispense from.

Cut the lemon and have it ready.

Business time.

Cut the tofu into 0.5 x 2 x 4 cm (¼ x ¾ x 1½ inch) rectangles and dust in the cornflour. It will likely still have liquid in it making the flour tacky, so do this at the last minute. Place the pieces on baking paper.

Heat the oil in a large, deep non-stick frying pan to 180–190°C (350–375°F).

Fry the rice paper pieces first, in batches of one or two. Each batch will take about 5 seconds, including turning, so be prepared. Use tongs to turn and place them on a paper towel to drain.

Fry the tofu in the same oil until golden on both sides, around 1 minute. Be careful as the crust may split if left too long.

Drain on paper towel too. I know ... WTF, no rack?! We already have the towel out so I am sticking to the process.

Place on a serving plate while still warm and sprinkle with the Chinese five-spice mix and chopped spring onions and serve.

Eat like this: hand + lettuce + rice crisp + tofu + cuke + spring onions + hoisin + lemon juice. Hand > mouth (avoid fingers).

Serves 4 as a snack

Sticky Maple Mustard Brussels

Glorious.

⅓ cup (80 ml) extra virgin olive oil
1 kg (2 lb 4 oz) baby
  brussels sprouts
1 garlic clove, smashed
¼ cup (70 g) white miso paste
1 tablespoon dijon mustard
3 tablespoons maple syrup
¼ cup (65 g) tahini
1 cup (260 g) Greek-style yoghurt
¼ cup (60 ml) lemon juice
1 tablespoon sesame seeds or
  Everything Bagel Seasoning from
  page 216, to sprinkle

OPTIONAL INGREDIENTS
ground Korean chilli

Like many a veg, brussels have historically been murdered in a vat of bubbling water, and extracted drowned, limp, grey-ish and closer in consistency to sick than anyone could stomach.

Their beauty can be found here: blistered in dry heat with a sweet marinade and spicy sprinkle, served on a heavenly cloud of tangy, creamy dressing thick enough to swipe through.

Preheat the oven to 200°C (400°F) fan-forced. Lightly oil a baking tray with 1 tablespoon of the olive oil.

Trim off the base of the brussels and cut them in half. Some leaves will come loose and that's fine – these become crispy and delicious little burnt cinders.

Combine the garlic, miso, mustard, the remaining olive oil and 2 tablespoons of the maple syrup in a large bowl. Add the brussels, including the extra brussels leaves, and toss well.

Scatter onto the baking tray and roast for 20 minutes, until charred and crispy. Let them cool a little while you make the dressing.

Combine the tahini, yoghurt, lemon juice and remaining maple syrup in a medium bowl and mix well.

Dollop this tangy stuff in the centre of a shallow serving bowl or plate. Place the slightly cooled brussels on top of the dressing and sprinkle with sesame seeds or Everything Bagel Seasoning.

This works really well with a fried egg. Or on a bowl of quinoa. If you want to beef it all up, you know, sans beef.

Serves 4 as a side

CRACKERS

3 cups (450 g) plain
    (all-purpose) flour
2 teaspoons fine salt
½ cup (125 ml) extra virgin olive oil
¼ cup (60 ml) Everything Bagel
    Seasoning from page 216

TOFFEE BRIE

1 cup (220 g) white
    (granulated) sugar
½ cup (125 ml) grape juice,
    or 1 cup seedless dark grapes,
    blended and strained
1 wheel of brie

OPTIONAL
an audience

Now, I don't quite know who needs to know this recipe compilation, but it is elevated and fancy AF.

The toffee is so 'fab & fun' (literally my mum's fave phrase of all time). You could be a total nut and switch out the grape juice for, you know, other grape juice like port or pinot.

The crackers are so artisanal you may as well splatter a little paint on your hands so you can throw in matter-of-factly that you 'had a little daub in the studio today while the dough was resting ...'

To make the crackers, combine the flour, salt, olive oil and ¾ cup (185 ml) water in a standmixer* fitted with the dough hook, and mix on medium speed until a smooth dough has formed, about 10 minutes.

Wrap in plastic wrap and place in the fridge to rest for 20 minutes.

Preheat the oven to 200°C (400°F) fan-forced. Line two baking trays with baking paper.

On a lightly floured surface, roll out tablespoon-sized chunks of dough to around 7 x 15 cm

(2¾ x 6 inches) and 3 mm (⅛ inches) thick.

Lay each cracker on a baking tray and scatter with Everything Bagel Seasoning. Gently press the seasoning in by covering the crackers with baking paper and pressing with your hand.

Bake the crackers for 5 minutes, swapping the tray positions halfway through cooking so that they bake evenly. They will be golden when ready.

Allow to cool before serving.**

For the toffee, in a small saucepan over medium–high heat, combine the sugar and juice then allow it to simmer on low WITHOUT STIRRING for about 15 minutes until it is beginning to darken.

Place the cheese in a heatproof dish or on a baking tray lined with baking paper and pour the toffee in a thin layer on top. The toffee will begin to harden as it cools on the cheese.

Allow it to set before serving.

If you have excess toffee, set some nuts in it on a tray lined

with baking paper. You can silence the kids with it (it does seal your teeth together for a spell).

---

* You can form this dough using your hands in a bowl if you don't have a standmixer.

** You can store the crackers in an airtight container in the pantry for up to 3 months.

Makes 20 crackers + 1 showy wheel

Nicy Cez

Part Niçoise, part Caesar.

The Golden Crouton

Eat pretty, dress pretty,
think pretty.

half a loaf of sourdough bread
6 tablespoons (120 ml) extra virgin olive oil
fine salt and freshly ground black pepper, to season
4 yellow/orange capsicums (peppers), cut in half, seeds and cores removed
2 brown onions, cut into wedges
2 garlic cloves, smashed with skins on

800 g (1 lb 12 oz) golden and green tomatoes (baby, small, medium and large)
¼ cup (7 g) loosely packed basil leaves
¼ cup (7 g) fresh oregano leaves
¼ cup (60 ml) red wine vinegar
1 large burrata

OPTIONAL INGREDIENTS
'stale' bread

It is very dictator-y of me to have a GOLDEN crouton salad that requires yellow, orange and green produce, but honestly – the important thing is that the tomatoes are fresh, ripe and in season.

Also, what kind of maniac has a recipe asking for half a loaf of sourdough?

Hi.

I always seem to have half a stale loaf, but don't let me stop you from getting a fresh loaf.

If I get to it before it turns into a rock, I trim the crusts and tear it up and put it in the freezer. Sometimes I turn it into breadcrumbs. Or you can wash it and blast it in a hot oven for 10 minutes, or until it crisps back up.*

Preheat the oven to 180°C (350°F) fan-forced. Line a baking tray with baking paper.

Tear the sourdough up into 3 cm (1¼ inch) chunks. In a bowl, toss the sourdough with 2 tablespoons of the olive oil and season with S+P.

Place on the tray and bake until golden, about 6 minutes. Set the croutons aside.

Place the capsicums cut-side down on the same baking tray. Place the onions and garlic around the capsicum. Drizzle with 1 tablespoon of the olive oil and sprinkle with some fine salt and freshly ground black pepper.

Bake for 20 minutes, until the edges have started to colour and everything has softened and become juicy. Remove and allow to cool.

Meanwhile, cut the tomatoes in a manner that suits them individually. Big ones thickly sliced, mediums cut into quarters, cherries halved and babies kept whole for pure mouth-bursting pleasure.

Cut the baked capsicums into quarters and squeeze the garlic out of its skin.

Pile the croutons, tomatoes, capsicum, garlic, onion and herbs on a big serving platter and drizzle with 3 tablespoons of the olive oil and the red wine vinegar. Toss it

about with your hands (or those funny wooden salad hands if you prefer – tongs are a bit too rough).

Plonk a room-temp burrata somewhere on the salad, pour some rosé and crack into this salad with abandon.

---

* Inspired by panzanella, which uses stale bread soaked in salad juices, but in this recipe I toast the bread.

Serves 4–6

Sweet Remy Slaw

Ugly is in the eye
of the beholder.

DRESSING
⅔ cup (165 g) mayonnaise
1½ tablespoons finely
   chopped cornichons
1 teaspoon capers, finely chopped
1 tablespoon lemon juice
1 tablespoon wholegrain mustard
2 teaspoons finely chopped
   flat-leaf parsley leaves
¼ teaspoon dried tarragon
sea salt flakes, to taste

THE REST
¼ green cabbage
2 tablespoons chervil
2 tablespoons honey
2 cups (500 ml) warm water
1 celeriac
1 green apple
1 tablespoon finely snipped chives
freshly ground black pepper,
   to taste
extra virgin olive oil, for drizzling

OPTIONAL INGREDIENTS
roast tarragon and lemon ch**ken
would be absurd with this

Celeriac is more glorious than potato when it comes to its Before and After story. Bulky, warty, tough and crusty turns into shredded, delicate, pale and tender. I'm not going to divulge which of these I find more attractive because it's personal, although I will say it's probably not what you think.

The remy – remoulade – is the dressing. It's quite traditional, but basically it's a tangy mustardy herby mayo. It often includes hot sauce, but I chose not to include that here.

Make the remoulade by mixing all the dressing ingredients together well. Store in a jar in the fridge until needed (it will keep for 3 days).

Wash and shred the cabbage and store it in an airtight container lined with paper towel in the fridge.

Rinse and pick the chervil and make the same little paper towel bedding in an airtight container for storing in the fridge.

Stir the honey and warm water together in a bowl until the honey dissolves. Allow it to cool. HOT TIP: honey water works better than lemon for preventing browning! And when making something sweet, it's nice not to have too much residual tang.

Get a big mixing bowl ready with three-quarters of the remoulade in the base.

Peel and julienne the celeriac and apple as close to serving time as possible. Dunk them in the honey water for 30 seconds, then pop them straight into the dressing.

Top with the cabbage and toss well. I like to keep some cabbage undressed – it makes a nice contrast to have both fresh snappy and deliciously dripping salad.

Arrange on a platter – if you haven't noticed I am much more prone to using platters than bowls when serving (unless I'm trying to keep something warm or prevent liquid from going everywhere). LOUD AND PROUD.

Decorate with chives, chervil, a crash landing of freshly ground black pepper and a lick of extra virgin olive oil.

Serves 4 as a side

200 g (4 oz) bean thread
   (glass) noodles
½ cup (15 g) coriander
   (cilantro) leaves
½ cup (15 g) shiso leaves
1 spring onion (scallion),
   green parts only, julienned –
   but I'll explain below
1 green papaya
2 carrots
3 Lebanese (short) cucumbers
1 zucchini (courgette)
¼ white cabbage or small wombok
1 cup (115 g) bean sprouts,
   hairy ends picked off
½ cup (75 g) salted peanuts,
   toasted and chopped

SAUCE
½ cup (125 ml) lime juice
½ cup (140 g) crunchy
   peanut butter
3 teaspoons sesame oil
¼ cup (125 ml) maple syrup
1½ tablespoons soy sauce
¼ cup (60 ml) hot water

OPTIONAL INGREDIENTS
chilli

There's a moment in your life when you become aware that you have repeated something so often with mild confidence and calm that you now slip into autopilot when faced with the task. Laundry. Critiquing. Astrology. For me, it's often dinner. This one sends me into a completely blissful trance.

Boil a jug of water.

Put the noodles in a heatproof bowl and cover with the boiling water. Leave them to cool. They should be soft and salad-perfect when done.

For the sauce, combine the lime juice, peanut butter, sesame oil, maple syrup and soy sauce in another bowl, then whisk everything together with the hot water.

Pick the coriander and shiso leaves and place in iced water to perk up.

Spring onions are fun to make all curly. The trick here is to cut the green bit into 7 cm (2¾ inch) lengths, then open the tube by cutting down one side. Place it flat on a board and thinly slice with the 'grain' as thin as you can. Place the strips in iced water and they will curl like crazy.

Shredding time.

Go slow, be meticulous, it will be far nicer to eat.*

The papaya will have green flesh and is great in this salad. Papaya has to be julienned fresh, but the carrots, cucumber, zucchini and cabbage can be done a day ahead. Just store them in the fridge in an airtight container lined with damp paper towel.

When you're ready to serve, place the spring onions and herbs on paper towel to dry off. Then, in a large bowl, style, plonk, twist, place and arrange the tendrils of drained noodles, papaya and veg. Top with the herbs, bean shoots, crunchy nuts and, of course, slaps of dressing.

Serves 6

---

* If it turns out you like this salad, I highly recommend investing in a julienne peeler.

Noodle Nut Salad

My version of meditation.

Tofu Larb

Make this ahead, take it to
a mate, take it to work.

2 tablespoons long-grain
  white rice
450 g (1 lb) firm tofu, drained
1 tablespoon extra virgin olive oil
100 g (3½ oz) cherry tomatoes,
  quartered
1 red shallot, thinly sliced
1 baby cos lettuce, leaves
  trimmed and rinsed
1 Lebanese (short) cucumber,
  thinly sliced
1 cup (30 g) Thai basil leaves
1 cup (20 g) mint leaves

GARLIC PASTE
3 garlic cloves, coarsely chopped
1 lemongrass stem, white and
  green parts, chopped
5 cm (2 inch) knob of ginger,
  peeled and chopped
2 spring onions (scallions),
  white and green parts
2 tablespoons peanut oil

DRESSING
½ cup (125 ml) lime juice
2 teaspoons soft brown sugar
1 bird's eye chilli
2 teaspoons fine salt

OPTIONAL INGREDIENTS
steamed rice

Quite possibly one of my favourite things in this book. It's larb's time to shine. And shine it does.

It's GREAT.

In a large, dry non-stick frying pan (I say large because you'll use it for the tofu later), toast the rice over high heat, tossing regularly, until golden brown. It should take around 5 minutes. Don't let it burn. Set aside to cool, then grind to a fine powder in a mortar and pestle.

For the paste, use a food processor or stick blender to blitz the garlic, lemongrass, ginger and spring onions with the peanut oil until they form a smooth paste.

Break up the tofu with your fingers and mix it with the garlic paste.

Over high heat in the same pan you used for the rice, fry the tofu in olive oil until it is fragrant and golden, around 10 minutes. Set aside to cool to room temp.

For the dressing, in the same food processor you used for the garlic paste – no need to wash it out – purée the lime juice, brown sugar, chilli and salt.

Combine the tofu, tomatoes, shallot and dressing in a bowl and toss well.

Serve with lettuce, cucumber, herbs and a sprinkling of the toasted rice.

Serves 2, or 4 in a banquet

French Frills

Petit micro baby
ingredients = fancy AF.

2 shallots, thinly sliced
½ cup (125 ml) extra virgin olive oil
1 tablespoon red wine vinegar
1 teaspoon dijon mustard
½ teaspoon freshly ground
   black pepper
2 bunches asparagus,
   ends trimmed
250 g (9 oz) green beans*
1 cup (155 g) peas
1 butter lettuce
½ cup (25 g) micro herbs   .

OPTIONAL INGREDIENTS
French fries would be appropriate

Frilly skirts of lettuce, tight perky veg, young and flirty herbs, barely dressed in a warm sweet tangy lick of oil and vinegar.

Are you there yet? Me too.

The idea with this one is to use baby/young everything.

And the dressing should be just-above-room-temp warm.

It's fresh but works well with rich stuff (fennel ragu I'm thinking of you) and is so moreish you'll want bread for post-munch swiping.

Fry the shallots in the olive oil in a small saucepan over low heat for 5 minutes. Take the pan off the heat and whisk in the red wine vinegar and dijon to combine. Allow to cool. Season with freshly ground black pepper.

Place the asparagus, beans and peas in a heatproof bowl. Pour boiling water from the kettle over the veg. Let them sit for 2 minutes, then refresh the veg by plunging them into a bowl of icy water.

Separate the lettuce leaves and add to the icy water. When you're ready to serve the salad, dry the veg and leaves off by draining on paper towel.

Halve the asparagus lengthways.

Arrange the salad on a platter, drizzle with the dressing and top with some micro herbs.

_____

* See my stance on topping and tailing on page 142.

Serves 4 as a side

1½ cups (330 g) brown rice
1 tablespoon finely chopped
  coriander (cilantro) stems,
  plus ½ cup (15 g) leaves,
  for topping
1 teaspoon fine salt
100 ml (3½ fl oz) extra virgin
  olive oil
1 brown onion, finely diced
2 tablespoons Mexican Seasoning
  (page 216)
3 garlic cloves, smashed
2 x 400 g (14 oz) tins black beans
½ cup (125 ml) vegetable stock

½ iceberg lettuce, shredded
1 cup (100 g) grated cheddar
½ cup (125 g) sour cream

SALSA ROSSO
4 tomatoes, coarsely chopped
¼ cup (60 ml) extra virgin
  olive oil
1 tablespoon finely grated
  lime zest
2 tablespoons lime juice
½ cup (15 g) coriander (cilantro)
  leaves and stems
1 teaspoon fine salt

GUAC
2 avocados, peeled and
  stones removed
2 tablespoons lime juice
1 tablespoon chopped
  spring onion (scallion)
½ teaspoon fine salt
2 teaspoons extra virgin olive oil

OPTIONAL INGREDIENTS
chilli powder and
pickled jalapeños

The inspo for this came from a dining establishment in the US – it's a chain, it's fast and, I won't lie, it's good.

Plus, carbs, protein, greens and flavour-loading are all a priority in our house. I'm partial to a bowl, my son is partial to a trough, my others are partial to scoop-feeding and DIYing condiments, so it hits all the right bones and buttons.

To make the salsa and the guac, blend separately in a food processor, then store in airtight containers in the fridge; they'll both keep overnight. For the guac, press baking paper down onto the top to prevent it browning.

Cook the brown rice according to the packet directions. If there are none, rinse well, then simmer over low heat in 3 cups (750 ml) of water with the lid off until the rice has absorbed the water, around 15–20 minutes. Pop a lid on it, remove from the heat and set aside for 10 minutes to finish cooking. Stir through the

coriander stems, salt and ¼ cup (60 ml) of the olive oil. This makes an irresistible snack and, honestly, it's how I fill up while making this. Carb and salt. Thanks.

Meanwhile, fry these delicious beans!

In a large frying pan over medium-high heat, sauté the onion in the remaining 2 tablespoons of olive oil until golden, around 5 minutes. Add the spice mix and the garlic and cook for a further 5 minutes, until really fragrant. Add the beans – including their juice! – and the stock and bring to simmering point. Reduce the heat to low and simmer for 10 minutes. It will thicken slightly, but this is a soupy bean mix, not dry.

Divide the rice, beans, lettuce, guac, salsa, cheese, sour cream and coriander leaves between individual serving bowls.

In my house things get optional after rice and beans, but that's the beauty of making your own bowl of stuff. You will like it.

Serves 4

Burrito Bowl

DIY fast food fix.

Peach & Panda Salad

Does not contain panda.

1 small lemon
1 teaspoon fine salt
1 teaspoon white
    (granulated)sugar
4 garlic cloves, peeled
    and crushed
1 cup (35 g) basil, leaves
    and tender stalks only
¼ cup (7 g) rosemary leaves or
    1½ tablespoons dried rosemary

1 cup (250 ml) extra virgin olive oil
½ cup (150 g) labne (see the Beet
    Falafel recipe on page 96 to
    make your own)
2 cups (100 g) baby salad leaves
3 peaches
2 tablespoons red wine vinegar

OPTIONAL INGREDIENTS
fresh baguettes

Disclaimer. When my friend Rob told me he had a killer salad – Peach & Panda – I was sold.

It sounded delicious.

Then he corrected me: 'No – labne, Lucy, labne.'

Hmm alright, I guess that's OK.

I've adapted it slightly and added one of my fave things: quick preserved lemon. I urge you to use this on other occasions too, such as under grilled veg.

Peel the lemon with a peeler (keep about 15 cm/6 inches of the peel). Hopefully the pith is thin; if not, trim as much off as possible. Then slice the lemon as finely as possible. Place the lemon on a platter in a single layer and sprinkle with salt and sugar. Set this aside for 30 minutes. It's a quick preserve.

In a small saucepan over low heat simmer the reserved lemon peel, the garlic, two-thirds of the basil (reserving some for garnish) and the rosemary in the olive oil for 20 minutes. You don't want it to bubble or sizzle, just extract flavour. Set aside to cool. It's a quick confit.

Assemble the salad by dolloping the lemons with labne.

Nestle baby salad leaves and the extra basil leaves everywhere and scatter with torn peaches.*

Dress liberally with the room-temp flavoured oil and the vinegar.

The lemons are tangy, sweet and sour, the leaves crisp and the labne creamy and fun.

A baguette is a worthy accessory to this one. Piling the fluffy bread with big wet mouthfuls is the ideal situation for this beautiful salad.

---

* The trick to tearing a peach is to half-cut and half-tear it when it has been pried away from the stone somewhat. Too much tear and the peach will be mush; too much cutting and it won't feel as rustic as you'd like. But sometimes cutting is the only option. Listen to your peach. It will tell you one way or another what it can do.

Serves 4

A Seriously Glistening Salad

Unbridled sparkly goodness.

1 tablespoon extra virgin olive oil
⅓ cup (90 g) salted butter, melted
½ cup (125 ml) honey
600 g (1 lb 5 oz) small carrots
    (orange, purple, white),
    scrubbed well, leaves trimmed
½ bunch thyme sprigs
head of garlic, halved across its
    fat belly with the skin on
2 oranges
5–6 baby beets, scrubbed well,
    leaves removed

½ cup (125 ml) hot water
fine salt and freshly ground
    black pepper, to taste
400 g (14 oz) tinned baby lentils,
    rinsed and drained
⅓ cup (75 g) goat's curd
50 g (1¾ oz) rocket (arugula)

SALAD DRESSING
1 tablespoon dijon mustard
⅓ cup (80 ml) extra virgin olive oil
2 tablespoons orange juice
    (reserved from the salad)
1 tablespoon red wine vinegar
2 tablespoons snipped chives
fine salt and freshly ground black
    pepper, to taste

OPTIONAL INGREDIENTS
other carbs

This salad should be glistening and bright in colour. The bright orange and purple should stay separate from the dark little spots of lentils and the glossy ghostly white of the goat's curd. If you over-toss it before serving you will end up with a murky toned pink wash from the beetroot everywhere.

It's a wintry rainbow of caramelised roots, perfect on its own or with a side of heavily buttered baguette, tossed with spaghetti or atop buttery couscous.

Preheat the oven to 200°C (400°F) fan-forced. Lightly oil a 40 x 50 cm (16 x 20 inch) deep baking tray with the extra virgin olive oil.

Combine the butter and the honey in a small mixing bowl.

Cut the carrots in half lengthways – or leave whole if thin – and place on the oiled tray. Add the thyme and garlic. Remove the peel from one of the oranges in strips and

add them to the tray. Pour the honey butter mixture over it all and toss well.

Cut the beets in sixths, place them on the tray and turn them over to coat.

Add ½ cup (125 ml) of hot water to the small mixing bowl you used for the honey butter and swirl it around to collect anything left in the bowl. Pour this over the veg.

Season well with a good crack of black pepper and a decent sprinkling of salt. Place the tray in the oven to roast for 20 minutes, or until caramelised.

Meanwhile, trim the remaining pith from the peeled orange and cut the flesh into segments. Juice the remaining orange and set the juice aside for the dressing.

Combine the dressing ingredients and season.

Remove the tray from the oven, add the lentils immediately, then allow it to cool slightly.

Before serving, top with the orange segments, crumbled goat's curd, a scrabble of rocket and the dressing.

Serves 4

Salads v. Sides

If a salad gets a sprinkle of something hot, does it immediately
become a side? Well, no, not if it's big ... these salads are pretty,
simple and delicious. Words to live by.

Serves 2-4

Asparagus, Parmy, Lemon, Crumb

2 bunches asparagus,
ends trimmed
1 tablespoon extra virgin olive oil
1 teaspoon fine salt
¼ cup (15 g) panko
breadcrumbs or stale bread
whizzed into crumbs
1 garlic clove, smashed
2 tablespoons finely
grated parmesan
1 tablespoon finely grated
lemon zest

Toss the asparagus in the olive oil and salt, then pan-fry over high heat in a medium frying pan (or on the grill/BBQ), tossing regularly until beginning to char, around 5 minutes.

Remove the asparagus and place on a serving plate.

Fry the breadcrumbs and garlic in the same frying pan on high heat until toasted, around 5 minutes.

Remove the pan from the heat and add the parmy and the zest. Mix well, then sprinkle it all over the asparagus and serve.

Radicchio, Blue Cheese, Walnut, Honey

2 cups (90 g) radicchio leaves, torn
60 g (2¼ oz) soft blue
cheese, chopped
¼ cup (90 ml) honey
1 tablespoon rosemary
leaves, bruised
2 tablespoons walnuts,
coarsely chopped
1 tablespoon red wine vinegar

Arrange the radicchio and cheese on a platter.

In a small saucepan over medium heat, warm the honey, rosemary and walnuts until just simmering, around 2 minutes. Add the red wine vinegar and remove from the heat. Drizzle this over the blue cheese and radicchio while still hot.

Beans, Tomato, Feta

1 garlic clove, smashed
500 g (1 lb 2 oz) green
beans, topped and tailed
and cut in half
400 g (14 oz) tinned
crushed tomatoes
½ tin (200 ml) of water
2 tablespoons extra virgin olive oil
fine salt and freshly ground black
pepper, to taste
50 g (1¾ oz) Greek-style feta,
crumbled

Preheat the oven to 200°C (400°F) fan-forced. Combine all the ingredients except the feta in an ovenproof dish, taste and season. Toss well. Cover tightly with foil or a lid. Bake for 1½ hours. Allow to cool, then sprinkle with the feta. It's also delicious warm.

Forever known as the day after, the last day
on earth, or the day before we begin again.

Is it the beginning of the week or the end?

Just like the answers to those perennial
questions, 'Who is the richest person?'
or 'Is chocolate actually nice?', it depends
on your perspective. No one really knows.

One thing is for certain: exactly like soup, eggs
have no hour or season … they are anytime.

Sunday Oeufs

In Hell

One egg each + one for the
pan, or the devil in this case.

300 g (10½ oz) potatoes, sliced
    into chunky shards, skins on
3 tablespoons extra virgin olive oil
1 brown onion, thinly sliced
1 red capsicum (pepper), seeds
    removed and thinly sliced
3 garlic cloves, thinly sliced
2 whole dried red chillies
1 teaspoon chilli flakes
½ teaspoon turmeric
1 teaspoon paprika
1 teaspoon fine salt
1 teaspoon dried oregano

⅔ cup (170 ml) tinned
    crushed tomatoes
5 eggs
2 tablespoons aioli
1 tablespoon Chilli Crisp
    (page 215)
1 lemon, cut into wedges

OPTIONAL INGREDIENTS
1 bird's eye chilli, sliced,
and finely chopped parsley

Is it shakshuka-ish? Yes. Do I prefer the term 'In Hell'? Yes. Purely because it makes me feel like a badass.

Yes, shakshuka is a GREAT word. Loosely meaning 'all mixed up', it's a perfect start to any haphazard day.

I once made a dish with so much capsicum in it that I had a reaction to the capsaicin and ended up with those insanely irritating disco legs that make you want to kick around in your sleep all night. The traditional recipe calls for chilli peppers, cayenne and paprika, so I like to arm myself with sourdough on the side or, in this case, throw in some cooked potatoes to soak things up a bit.

It becomes a little like patatas bravas then, too. I like to fantasy continent-hop while at my kitchen bench, especially when I'm already on my way to Hell.

Boil the spuds in salted water until tender, 15 minutes, then drain.

In a large deep frying pan, heat 2 tablespoons of the olive oil over medium heat. Sauté the onion and capsicum for 5 minutes, until the onions are beginning to turn golden. Add the garlic and dried chillies and sauté for a further 2 minutes.

Add in all the remaining spices, salt and oregano and stir until it is well mixed.

Then toss in the potatoes and the remaining 1 tablespoon of olive oil and stir well. Combine the tomatoes and ⅔ cup (170 ml) of water and pour that in too. Simmer for 5 minutes, until it begins to reduce slightly.

Make some little wells with the back of a spoon for the eggs. You can evenly space them for serving or, if you're me, deliberately cluster them together – because being the devil's advocate is par for the course in this one.

Crack in the eggs and reduce the heat to low. Do not stir once the eggs are in. Allow them to poach for 5–7 minutes, covering for the last 3 minutes.

Serve with aioli, Chilli Crisp oil and bird's eye chilli … or don't. Definitely add the activity of lemon squeezing to the agenda.

Serves 4

In Heaven

A heavenly scenario that is
only as pretty as it looks.

1 leek, white and pale green parts
    sliced into 5 mm (¼ inch) rounds
4 thyme sprigs
2 garlic cloves, thinly sliced
¼ cup (60 g) salted butter
1 tablespoon extra virgin olive oil
1 cup (45 g) firmly packed
    spinach leaves
¾ cup (185 ml) thick
    (double) cream
½ cup (50 g) finely
    grated parmesan

1 tablespoon dijon mustard
¼ teaspoon ground nutmeg
fine salt and freshly ground
    black pepper, to taste
4 eggs

OPTIONAL INGREDIENTS
peace

The calm, the coddled, the soft and the gentle. Quiet and creamy, eggs In Heaven are decadent and beautiful. Even more rewarding if you are able to wake at dawn, fresh from rest, pad out to the garden to harvest leaves straight from the rich soil, then skim the cream solids from the top of a wooden pail of thick cow's milk. Meander to the coop to collect the eggs from between warm straw and the fluffy underside of a fat hen, and casually return to the kitchen with the first rays of sunshine hitting your back just as the kettle begins to whistle.

In. Your. Blogging. Dreams.

In our house, this delightful little scenario is subbed out for things like a landmine Lego collection, conflict management (forget resolution), and a general blinking response to all the activity.

But get that pan to the table with a hopefully-still-warm cup of tea, and the escalator to Heaven will appear.

Sweat the leeks with the thyme, garlic, butter and oil for about 10 minutes in a large frying pan with the lid on, over very low heat.

Add the spinach in an even layer on top, and cover the pan again for another 2 minutes, until it has wilted.

In a small bowl, combine the cream, parmesan, dijon and nutmeg and season well with S+P. Make four little egg wells in the spinach, then pour in the cream mixture.

Allow the cream to heat up to steaming, then crack the eggs into the wells.

Cover with a lid for 5 minutes, then remove the lid and continue to cook for a further 3 minutes, until the whites are cooked but the yolks are runny.

Season to taste, and serve with buttered toasted sourdough baguette (which you made fresh this morning at about 4 am, in a wood oven).

Serves 2

½ butternut pumpkin (squash)
⅓ cup (80 ml) extra virgin olive oil
1 teaspoon fine salt
1 tablespoon shichimi
   togarashi (Japanese
   chilli seasoning)
1 bunch kale, tough ribs
   discarded, leaves and tender
   ribs coarsely chopped
2 tablespoons lemon juice
1 cup (200 g) quinoa
1 avocado
4 radishes

8 eggs
¼ cup (60 ml) white vinegar
2 cups (320 g) frozen
   edamame beans, thawed
1 cup cauliflower Curry Pickle
   from page 215
1 cup (250 g) sauerkraut (I used
   a red one because – rainbow)
4 tablespoons smoked almonds,
   coarsely chopped
½ cup mixed herbs – dill, flat-leaf
   parsley, coriander (cilantro),
   all picked
1 nori sheet, finely sliced

DRESSING
½ garlic clove, smashed
1 tablespoon honey
1 tablespoon wholegrain mustard
1 tablespoon lemon juice
½ teaspoon fine salt
⅓ cup (80 ml) extra virgin olive oil

OPTIONAL INGREDIENTS
a cult – if you're unsure,
call your dad

This recipe could be called Buddha Brunch, Rainbow Bright or Golden Sunshine – but cult seems more appropriate because I feel like we've all signed up for this situation at least once.

Whether it's because of the probiotic kraut, the massaged kale, or the nuts, or just because it has the word 'bowl' in it as if that's part of the actual ingredients, you just know it's going to be a power packet of goodness.

Preheat the oven to 200°C (400°F) fan-forced.

Peel and cube the pumpkin into 1 cm (½ inch) squares and toss in a large bowl with 2 tablespoons of the olive oil, the salt and the togarashi. Place on a baking tray and bake for 20 minutes, until caramelised. Set aside to cool and remember to be #grateful when you go to grab a snack and this is in the fridge.

Place the kale in a bowl, add the remaining olive oil and the lemon juice and massage the leaves until they relax. Yes. You have to do this. Set this aside also.

Cook the quinoa according to the packet directions. Allow it to cool.

Peel the avocado, remove the stone and quarter, then place in a bowl of icy water.

Shave the radish into the avocado bowl so it can curl and crisp up, then dry the wet veg on paper towel.

For the dressing, place the garlic, honey, mustard, lemon juice, salt and olive oil in a jar and shake it, or whisk together if you don't have a jar (note to self: start keeping jars).

Poaching eggs: don't be frightened, just be bold. In a deep non-stick saucepan, bring 4 cups (1 litre) of water and the vinegar to a steady simmer. Crack the eggs into a cup and plop them carefully in one at a time. Use a slotted spoon to gently nudge them away from the base of the pan to prevent them sticking. When the water comes back to a simmer, turn the heat down and allow the eggs to poach for 5 minutes. Remove with a slotted spoon.

Assembly of this is crucial: it's less about flavour (which is guaranteed) and more about aesthetics. And

don't let ANYONE tell you it doesn't matter – eating with your eyes is an important part of the process, whether you're zen AF or completely superficial. It's called being present. Nestle each ingredient into small piles into the bowl, so you end up with a giant group hug – which in my opinion is the ONLY appropriate place for one.

This makes the most pretentiously fantastic desk lunch too: just swap out the poached egg for a freshly boiled soft egg (fridge to boiling water @ 6 minutes) and transfer in the shell to work.

Serves 4

Cult Bowl

Mum used to say 'eat the rainbow' – she'd melt.

Silky Folds Taco

Post-party peacekeeper.

2 cups (400 g) tinned corn
     kernels, drained
1 coriander (cilantro) stem, leaves
     picked and stems finely diced
2 spring onions (scallions),
     thinly sliced
⅓ cup (80 ml) extra virgin olive oil
10 eggs
2 tablespoons milk
1 avocado
1 lime

pinch of fine salt
1 tablespoon green habanero
     sauce (or any chilli sauce),
     or to taste
12 mini tortillas
1 cup (100 g) grated cheddar
2½ tablespoons salted butter
fine salt and freshly ground
     black pepper, to taste
30 g (1 oz) large leaf rocket
     (arugula)

OPTIONAL INGREDIENTS
extra chilli sauce

If you have flatmates and you've been lazy about your share of shopping/cleaning/partying, etc., make this for them with a big pot of coffee/chocolate and almost all will be forgiven. I do it for my flatmates* occasionally, so I can vouch for this.

Preheat the oven to 200°C (400°F) fan-forced. Line a large baking tray with baking paper.

Fry the corn, coriander stems and spring onion in a large frying pan with 1 tablespoon of the olive oil over medium heat for 5 minutes. Set aside.

Meanwhile, crack the eggs into a bowl, add milk and whisk to combine. Set aside.

Remove the skin and stone from the avocado, finely dice the flesh and place into a bowl. Zest half the lime, juice the same half and add both to the avocado. Cut the remaining half of the lime into wedges and set aside. Season

the avo and lime with a pinch of salt, then stir in 2 tablespoons of olive oil and the chilli sauce, to taste. Add the cooled corn to the avocado mixture and combine.

Lay the tortillas out on the tray and sprinkle the grated cheese on top. Place in the oven for 5 minutes, or until the cheese has melted.

Time to cook the eggs. I advise doing this in two batches, but if you can fit it all in one go, do it! Over medium heat in a large non-stick frying pan, add the butter and remaining olive oil. Once the butter is starting to sizzle, add the eggs and fold gently until just set, around 5 minutes.

Top the cheesy tortillas with some of the egg, then the corn and avocado salsa. Season with salt and freshly ground black pepper. Add the coriander leaves and rocket and serve with lime wedges.

* My flatmates are thankless jerks most of the time – they always want me to watch when they learn to do something new, but never pay attention to me for longer than a sentence. Oddly though, I am so in love with them that I often dream about them, I buy them new undies, and I will query them when they demand money only sometimes.

Serves 6 (makes 12)

French Rarebit

Just a cute girly brunch.

4 eggs, plus four extra for
    fried eggs on top if you want
    to go hardcore
2 cups (500 ml) single
    (pure) cream
2 teaspoons onion powder
2 teaspoons garlic powder
fine salt, to season
1 sourdough loaf (around
    10 slices)
⅓ cup (90 g) salted butter
⅔ cup (100 g) plain
    (all-purpose) flour

6 teaspoons wholegrain mustard
4 teaspoons mustard powder
2 teaspoons cayenne pepper
1¾ cups (435 ml) ale,
    warmed and set aside
2 cups (200 g) grated cheddar
2 cups (200 g) grated gruyere
2 cups (500 g) sauerkraut or
    caramelised onions

OPTIONAL INGREDIENTS
eggs on top

**It's when French toast and Welsh
rarebit become inseparable bffs:
sourdough soaked in glorious egg
and cream, topped with tangy
kraut and Welsh rarebit, then
grilled to bubbling perfection.**

**It's a brunch vibe (or linner), but
make it tough and cool.**

Preheat the oven to 180°C (350°F)
fan-forced. Line a baking tray
with foil or baking paper.

Whisk the eggs, cream and onion
and garlic powders in a dish or
shallow bowl that will fit all the
slices of bread. Season with salt.
Place the bread into the dish and
allow it to soak for 10–15 minutes
each side.

Meanwhile, melt the butter* in a
heavy-based medium saucepan
over medium heat until it begins
to foam. Add the flour, mustard
and spices and stir well to form a
paste. Add the warm ale in batches
of ¼ cup (60 ml), stirring until
smooth after each addition. Add
the cheeses and stir until melted
through, then set this rarebit mix
aside to cool.

Place the soaked bread on the
baking tray, carefully drizzling
all the remaining eggy cream
mixture over the slices to use it
up. Bake in the oven until crisp,
around 25 minutes. Remove the
tray from the oven and preheat
the grill/broiler.

Top each piece of bread with
kraut or onions, then the rarebit
mix, spreading it out as much as
possible. Place the tray under
a hot grill so that it can bubble
and caramelise.

Now, if you want to be hardcore,
fry a couple of runny sunny-side-
up eggs and put them on top too.

Serve hot. Probably in this case
with more beer, because when
in Wales, Paris, Rome …

---

* If you are cooking this book chapter
by chapter then you will have made the
Vegemite butter on page 16. This recipe
is a GREAT use for any leftovers. Normal
butter is fine, but if you need an excuse
to make the Vegemite version then this
is a good one.

**Serves 5–10 depending on how
hardcore you are**

700 g (1 lb 9 oz) tomatoes, big
    and small, lovely and ripe
⅓ cup (80 ml) extra virgin olive oil
2 tablespoons red wine vinegar
2 small garlic cloves, crushed
1 teaspoon white
    (granulated) sugar
125 g (4½ oz) tomato passata
    (puréed tomatoes)
1 teaspoon sea salt flakes

CRUMBLE TOPPING
1 cup (70 g) torn stale bread
    (roughly 1 cm/½ inch chunks)
1 cup (100 g) grated cheddar
½ cup (75 g) plain
    (all-purpose) flour
1 tablespoon finely chopped
    thyme leaves
½ cup (120 g) cold salted
    butter, cubed

EGGS
9 eggs
¼ cup (60 ml) thick
    (double) cream, cold
1 tablespoon wholegrain mustard
2 tablespoons finely
    snipped chives
1 tablespoon salted butter

OPTIONAL
bellinis, obvs

**I think ripe tomatoes are my
weakness. I am addicted to
them. I can have a shopping list
with absolutely no mention of
tomatoes, and then I will see one,
or a punnet, and immediately my
cooking plans change. An oxheart
can overthrow an entire menu.**

Preheat the oven to 220°C (425°F)
fan-forced.

Slice the big toms and chop the
little ones in half. Place the sliced
tomatoes evenly into the bottom
of a 23 cm (9 inch) ovenproof dish
or frying pan.

Toss the remaining toms in a bowl
with the olive oil, red wine vinegar,
garlic, sugar, passata and salt.
Mix them well. Scatter these
tomatoes on top of the sliced
toms in the dish.

Place this in the oven to bake for
20 minutes, until bubbling and
beginning to caramelise.

Meanwhile, make the crumble
topping. Combine the bread,
cheddar, flour and thyme in

a bowl. Work the butter into the
mixture by squishing it in with your
fingers. When you get pea-size
chunks, stop.

Remove the tomatoes from the
oven and dollop the crumble
mixture over the top unevenly,
leaving a few gaps, then return
the dish to the oven to continue
cooking for a further 20 minutes,
until the top is golden and crisp
and the toms are beginning to
bubble around the edge.

About 15 minutes before finishing,
whisk together the eggs, cream,
mustard and half the chives.

Heat the butter in a large non-
stick frying pan over medium
heat until it begins to foam, about
1 minute. Pour the egg mixture
into the pan.

As the eggs begin to catch on the
edges of the pan, gently pull them
into the centre using a heatproof
silicone spatula. Continue stirring
the eggs until they have just set,
about 5–7 minutes. Remove from
the heat.

Top the eggs with the remaining
chives and serve hot with the
tomato crumble.

Serves 4

Tommy Crumble & Mustard Scram

This whole thing just screams brunch.

Crispy Edge

Appropriate 24/7.

½ cup (125 ml) vegetable oil
4 garlic cloves, thinly sliced
1 bunch water spinach,* cut into
   10 cm (4 inch) pieces, leaves
   and stems separated
½ teaspoon soft brown sugar
4 spring onions (scallions),
   thinly sliced, white and
   green parts separate
2 teaspoons sesame oil
1 teaspoon mushroom
   oyster sauce

4 eggs
2 cups (370 g) steamed white rice
½ teaspoon finely grated ginger
1 bird's eye chilli, thinly sliced

OPTIONAL INGREDIENTS
doubanjiang chilli paste

Crispy, sticky, saucy, spicy, gooey, chewy.

This has all the elements of the ideal any-time-of-day meal.

It's a perfect bowl of things and should be made as a priority.

It does involve a spitting oil situation, so don't be brazen or slack about the egg bit.

Heat 1 tablespoon of the vegetable oil in a non-stick wok over high heat, then add the garlic and cook, stirring, until golden, 1 minute. Add the stems of the water spinach with the brown sugar and the whites of the spring onion. After 1 minute, add the leafy ends of the spinach and the sesame oil and toss well. Stir in the mushroom oyster sauce and 1 tablespoon of water. Cover to steam for 2 minutes, then toss well and set aside. Keep warm.

Wipe out the wok with some paper towel. Place a large plate at the ready on your benchtop.

Heat the remaining oil over high heat until hot. Add the eggs one at a time, keeping separate if

possible. Allow the eggs to fry for 2 minutes, or until the edges are crisping. Remove the eggs and pop them on the plate while you carefully pour out all but 1 tablespoon of oil. Place the eggs back in the wok to continue cooking for 1 minute more, until the whites are cooked and the centres are still runny.

To serve, fill the individual bowls with rice, then add the eggs and water spinach mixture. Top with the ginger, chilli and the remaining spring onion. Add a drizzle of the water spinach sauce.

_____

* Water spinach chit chat: you can swap this out for any deep green stalky side: bok choy, broccolini, English spinach, Chinese broccoli (gai lan) or silverbeet. I lunged at the opportunity to cook water spinach when I saw it available, and quite possibly this entire recipe owes its existence to it. It's fun and vibrant and the stalks are tubular, meaning they fill with flavour. I love the crunch of this veg.

Serves 2

Chilaquiles

Real talk: I'm really not that
much of a frittata person.

8 eggs
¼ cup (60 ml) milk
1 tablespoon salted butter
2 tablespoons extra virgin olive oil
1 white onion, finely chopped
1 tablespoon finely chopped
    coriander (cilantro) stems,
    leaves reserved
1 green capsicum (pepper),
    finely diced
2 garlic cloves, finely chopped
1 teaspoon garlic powder
1 teaspoon onion powder
1 cup (30 g) corn chips

½ cup (50 g) grated cheddar
½ cup (65 g) grated mozzarella
⅓ cup (30 g) grated
    smoked cheddar
1 avocado, peeled and stone
    removed, sliced
2 radishes, cut into matchsticks
¼ teaspoon smoked paprika
    or cayenne pepper
1 tablespoon jalapeño sauce
    (or mole)

OPTIONAL INGREDIENTS
a sister in LA, though it helps

This is as close as I'll happily get to a frittata – I don't really like brown burnt eggs (she says, a page after telling you to crispy fry them). It begins with the concept of a frittata but delivers a texture combo of crispy corn chip and soft creamy eggs that is just perfect.

This dish makes me happy. Maybe it's because my sister made it for me one morning in LA after I hadn't seen her for too long. Maybe it's because it's so good.

Preheat the oven to 200°C (400°F) fan-forced.

Whisk the eggs in a lazy fashion in a bowl with the milk.

Melt the butter and olive oil in a large ovenproof frying pan over medium heat until foaming. Add the onion, coriander stems and capsicum and sauté for 3 minutes, until soft. Add the garlic, garlic powder and onion powder and cook for a further 4 minutes.

Pour in the eggs and allow the edges to bubble and begin to set for 1 minute.

Place the pan in the oven for 5 minutes, then remove it to add the corn chips and cheese. Sprinkle the cheeses above and below the corn chips. (Cheese layering – like on pizza – is not a blank-faced dump and run. You need to poke things under and out. Cheese needs to be able to flow and follow its natural stream-like journey.)

Place the pan back in the oven for 5–10 minutes, until the cheese has melted and is bubbling – keep an eye on it so the chips don't burn.

Decorate this protein pancake with the avo, snappy radish, coriander leaves, a shadow of paprika and a dribble of jalapeño sauce.

2, 4, 6, 8 … you know the drill.

Serves 4

500 g (1 lb 2 oz) baby white
  potatoes, quartered
200 g (7 oz) green beans,
  tops removed
1 fennel bulb
1 red onion
6 radishes
1 cos lettuce
1 head garlic, cut in half
  horizontally with skin left on, cut
  edges drizzled with olive oil, plus
  4 extra garlic cloves, smashed

¼ cup (60 g) salted butter
100 ml (3½ fl oz) extra virgin
  olive oil
1 small sourdough loaf
6 cold eggs
¼ cup (40 g) cornichons, chopped
1 tablespoon baby capers
¼ cup (40 g) pitted kalamata
  olives, sliced
1 teaspoon finely chopped
  oregano leaves

1½ tablespoons chopped
  dill sprigs
1 tablespoon basil leaves
1 tablespoon finely snipped chives
2 teaspoons lemon juice
1 tablespoon mayonnaise
1 oxheart tomato, thickly sliced

OPTIONAL INGREDIENTS
nothing – it's complete

If you've ever been confused by the dress code 'smart casual', imagine eating this on a sunny vine-adorned balcony overlooking some kind of vista/plain/ocean. There could be a sweater over the shoulders. It's that vibe. I've also eaten this in a tracksuit and it's been brilliant – so just use it as inspiration, not a demand.

Preheat the oven to 170°C (325°F) fan-forced.

Simmer the spuds in a large saucepan of salted water for 13 minutes, until tender, then add the beans and simmer for 2 minutes more. Drain and set aside to cool.

Meanwhile, trim and shave the fennel, red onion and radishes and place in icy water. They will repay you by being vibrant and bouncy when you serve them. Trim the lettuce and pop the leaves in icy water too.

Join the cut halves of the garlic back together and wrap in foil. Place in the oven and roast for 15 minutes, until soft. Cool, then squeeze the cloves from the skins.

In a small saucepan over medium heat, heat the butter with 2 tablespoons of the olive oil and the remaining 4 garlic cloves for 2 minutes, until bubbling. Set aside.

Line a tray with foil and then baking paper. Slice the bread into eight slices – but don't go all the way through. Place the loaf on the tray and brush or pour the garlic butter between the slices as much as possible. Wrap tightly in the foil and pop in the oven for 20 minutes. When the garlic bread is done, remove it from the oven but keep it warm. (If you prefer crispier garlic bread, open the top after 20 minutes and allow it to cook for a further 10 minutes.)

Bring enough water to the boil in a saucepan to submerge 6 eggs. Use a pin to pierce the fatter end of each egg, then lower them into the water slowly so they don't crack. Boil for 6 minutes for jammy eggs.* Peel under cold running water and place in a bowl of cold water until ready to serve.

In a small bowl, combine 1 tablespoon of the olive oil, the cornichons, capers, olives, oregano and 2 teaspoons of the dill. Set aside.

In a small blender, process the roasted garlic with the remaining dill, remaining olive oil, basil, chives, lemon juice and mayonnaise until green and vibrant.

Layer and stack the tomato, beans, leaves, curly bouncy veg (dried on paper towel) and potatoes. Throw on a few spoonfuls of the olive mix and a dollop of green mayo.

Serve with hot garlic bread and a penchant for good times.

---

* Due to altitude this may not be the correct timing for jammy eggs in the south of France!

Serves 4 snappy customers

Eggs Niçoise
Breakfast Salad

You could be drinking tea
or pinot gris – your call.

Green Eggs & Jam Tart

An all-in-one, crispy-edged
condiment carrier.

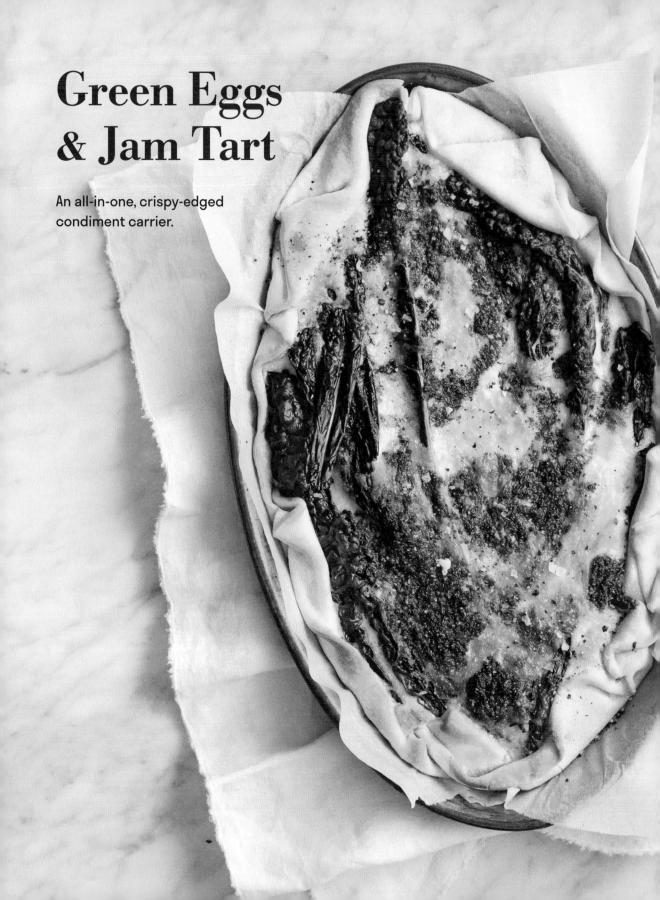

2 sheets ready-made
   frozen shortcrust pastry
150 g (5½ oz) cavolo nero
   (tuscan kale)
2 tablespoons extra virgin olive oil,
   plus more for brushing
1 garlic clove, crushed
¼ cup (60 ml) onion jam
8 eggs
1 tablespoon thick (double) cream

1 cup (100 g) grated cheddar
fine salt and freshly ground
   black pepper
2 tablespoons Scrap Pesto
   from page 216

OPTIONAL INGREDIENTS
a quick zest of lemon would
be great

A picnic crowd-pleaser.

You can swap out the cav nero for any other dark leafy green, and mix up the jam too – I have used store-bought onion jam, but tomato or chilli would be equally delicious.

The faint sweetness of the onion jam is perfect with creamy cheesy eggs swirled with vibrant green pesto and robust foliage.

This can be dinner, lunch or breakfast, easily eaten by fork or by hand.

Thaw the shortcrust.

Preheat the oven to 200°C (400°F) fan-forced.

Rinse the leafy greens and shake them dry. Trim any tough ribs off the leaves. Younger tender ribs can be left whole, or just trim the base if it is a more tender bunch.

In a large non-stick frying pan, heat 2 tablespoons of olive oil over high heat. Add the garlic and cavolo nero and stir-fry for 1–2 minutes, until the greens have only just begun to char and wilt. Remove from the heat and set aside.

Line a baking dish with baking paper – I have used an oval dish 20 x 35 cm (8 x 14 inches).

Place the two sheets of shortcrust pastry into the dish, overlapping at the centre.

Use your fingers to press the pastry together and seal it along the join.

Spread the onion jam onto the pastry and then top with the wilted garlicky greens.

In a bowl, whisk together the eggs and cream until well combined. Add the cheese and season well.

Pour this mixture on top of the greens. Dot small amounts of pesto onto the egg mixture, then swirl it about gently with the back of a spoon.

Fold and tuck the excess pastry edges around the egg mixture, then brush with the extra olive oil.

Place into the oven to bake for 20 minutes, or until the centre is just set.

Serves 4

Hash & Egg Muffins

Good and greasy washed down
with black coffee.

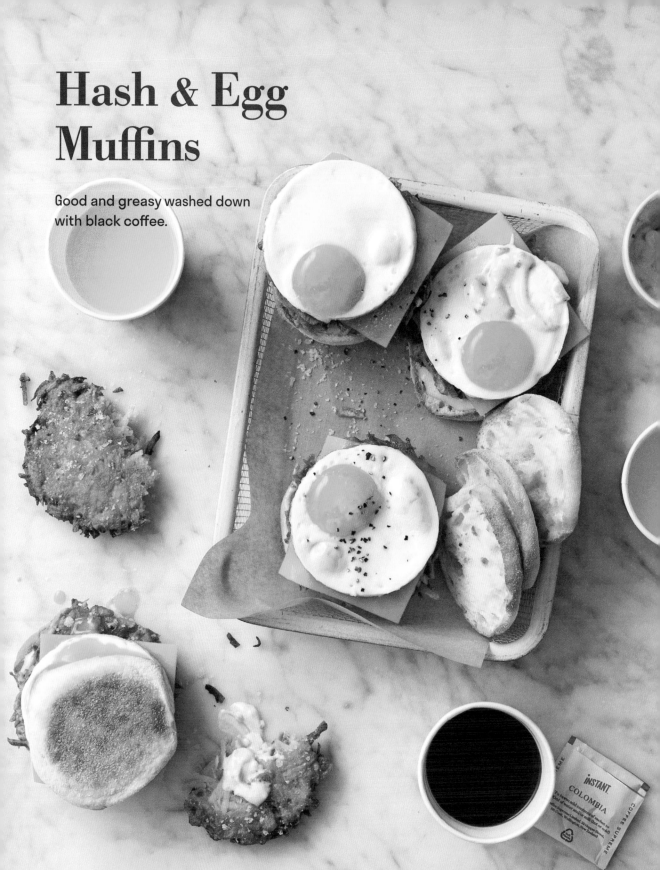

4 eggs
4 English muffins
4 slices American cheese

SAUCE
¾ cup (185 g) mayo
¼ cup (65 g) gherkin relish
1½ teaspoons onion powder
1½ teaspoons garlic powder
½ teaspoon cayenne pepper
4 teaspoons American mustard
2 teaspoons white wine vinegar

HASH
800 g (1 lb 12 oz) potatoes
2 eggs, lightly whisked
2 tablespoons cornflour
  (cornstarch)
1 teaspoon garlic powder
1 teaspoon paprika
1 teaspoon fine salt
½ cup (125 ml) canola oil

OPTIONAL INGREDIENTS
instant coffee, but the good kind

There's nothing wrong with food from fast food chains – especially the homemade version, with better ingredients and a much slower, more pain-in-the-ass process than driving through. I worked at one once. There were a few free upsizes for mates. While I was never provided with a fitting uniform, I stayed long enough to garner some hilarious stories, glean some food science insights and swish the special sauce enough times like a sommelier to grab the tasting notes ... for this very day!

Combine all the sauce stuff together. I know ... that's it. I could fluff it out with 'in a bowl' and 'with a spoon' and 'store in a blah blah' – actually, just store in a jar in the fridge for a week. But that's it. Mix. Store. Brains.

For the hash, peel and grate the potatoes, place in a clean tea towel and squeeze out the excess moisture. Then, in a large bowl, combine the spud with the eggs, cornflour, garlic powder, paprika and salt.

Divide into eight portions and shape each into a 10–12 cm (4–4½ inch) round, 1 cm (½ inch) thick. Place them on a tray lined with baking paper and freeze for 20 minutes.

Heat the canola oil in a large frying pan over medium heat, then add the hash in batches and fry for 5 minutes, turning once, until golden on both sides.

Set them aside in a warm place (a commercial hotbox would be ideal).

Lightly grease a large non-stick frying pan and heat over medium heat. Add the eggs one at a time using a greased fancy egg ring for full fast-food immersion (or hack that by using the largest ring of a slice of onion that is cut at least 1 cm/½ inch wide). Cover with a lid and cook until the entire egg is just set. You can do a runny yolk here of course if you wish, it's your T-shirt.

Meanwhile, split and lightly toast the muffins under the grill until lightly golden.

Spread the heel (this is what the fast-food industry calls the bun bum – you're welcome) with sauce. Top with a hash, a slice of cheese, then an egg. Whack the lid on.

I like to wrap mine, take it to the car and drive around the block while eating it for full effect.

Drinks pairing: pulpless orange juice watered down to about two-thirds and consumed out of a paper cup that has a really faint aroma of detergent.

Serves 4

2 cups (320 g) rice flour
½ cup (125 ml) coconut cream
1 egg
2 teaspoons turmeric powder
1¼ tablespoons peanut oil
pinch of fine salt
1 cup (20 g) Vietnamese
mint leaves
1 cup (20 g) mint leaves
1 cup (20 g) shiso leaves
1 coral lettuce, leaves picked
½ onion, cut into thin rings

¼ pumpkin (squash), peeled and
seeds removed, cut into 2 cm
(¾ inch) cubes, roasted at 220°C
(425°F) fan-forced on a greased
baking tray for 20 minutes
1 cup (115 g) bean sprouts
2 cups (200 g) tinned corn
kernels, drained
Basic Pickle, from page 215
chilli sauce, to serve
mushroom oyster sauce, to serve
1 lime, cut into eight thin wedges

OPTIONAL INGREDIENTS
jammy eggs, and iced coffee
made with sweetened
condensed milk

Another activity piece. Pick a bit of this, chopstick in some of that, grab a few of those, wrap in a leaf, munch. And it's the perfect user-upper of stuff in the fridge: old roast veg, floppy things, or pantry bits like tinned corn.

It's a really fun thing to make for dinner (and doubles as a brunch scenario). You could definitely add chopped jammy eggs and hit people with an iced coffee made with sweetened condensed milk.

I mean, I'd come back, even if you didn't want me to.

In a large bowl, combine the rice flour, coconut cream, egg, turmeric powder, 1 tablespoon of the peanut oil, a big pinch of salt and 2⅓ cups (580 ml) of water. Whisk well, then allow to rest for 30 minutes.

Pick all the herbs and lettuce leaves and let them get super perky by popping them in an ice bath with plenty of water. They need about 15–20 minutes here. Place them on paper towel to dry off a bit before serving.

Pancake-making of any variety is a committed event. This one is no different.

Arrange all the fillings in little vessels near the stove at the ready. This is a game called 'ultimate mise en place' and it will change the way you cook.

Heat the remaining 1 teaspoon of peanut oil in a large non-stick frying pan over high heat and add ⅓ cup (80 ml) of pancake batter. Immediately swirl the pan – applying serious wrist-twirling skills – to stretch the pancake out across the surface. Thin and crispy is what you're aiming for, but a little chunk won't hurt anyone.

While the batter is still wet, add the toppings: raw onion slices, roast pumpkin, bean sprouts and corn – a sprinkle (2 tablespoons) of each.

While the first pancake is cooking, stir the batter in the bowl so it stays thoroughly mixed. The pancake will take around 6 minutes to crisp and brown. Lift one edge to check the doneness and if it looks great then fold it in half and slide it onto a plate.

Onto the next pancake!

Serve with lettuce, herbs, pickles and condiments like chilli sauce and mushroom oyster sauce. Pickle juice is also a great tangy addition, along with a little wedge of lime.

Makes 8

Vietnamese Pancakes (Bánh Xèo)

Flex those wrist muscles, friends.

Anytime Eggs

Egg talk.

I use eggs from the fridge. Before boiling, use a pin and pierce the fatter end of each egg, then lower the eggs into the water slowly so they don't crack. Boil for the designated time. If you are peeling, do so under cool running water as it helps lift the membrane and the shell. If you are making ahead and want lovely, round, not flat-sided eggs, then place them in a container of water to bob about in the fridge.

Each recipe serves 2.

Grated Hard Egg Salad

1 tablespoon softened salted butter
4 slices sourdough bread, toasted
2 tablespoons goat's curd
¼ cup (35 g) frozen baby peas, thawed
¼ cup (5 g) mint leaves, chopped
2 teaspoons extra virgin olive oil
2 x 12-minute eggs

1 tablespoon finely grated lemon zest
1 tablespoon mayo
sea salt flakes and freshly ground black pepper, to taste

Apply the butter to the toast. Top this with swipes of goat's curd.

In a small bowl, crush the peas with a fork and mix in the mint and oil to combine.

Spoon this over the goat's curd.

Exciting bit: peel the hard-boiled eggs and grate them on top of each piece of toast from dizzying heights, fluffy and powder-like. Zest the lemon over the eggs.

Drizzle with mayo and add loads of sea salt and freshly ground black pepper.

Asparagus with Curried Gribiche

4 x 8-minute eggs
1 tablespoon capers,
    coarsely chopped
½ shallot, minced
4 cornichons, coarsely chopped
1 tablespoon dill,
    coarsely chopped
1 tablespoon flat-leaf parsley
    leaves, coarsely chopped
1 teaspoon dijon mustard
1 tablespoon lemon juice
1 tablespoon finely grated
    lemon zest
1 tablespoon white wine vinegar
1 teaspoon curry powder
sea salt flakes and freshly ground
    black pepper, to taste
1 bunch of asparagus,
    ends trimmed, blanched
    and finely chopped
1 tablespoon extra virgin olive oil,
    plus extra for drizzling
4 slices Polish rye, toasted
    and buttered
2 tablespoons chervil leaves,
    chopped

Peel and roughly chop the eggs and place in a bowl. Add the capers, shallot, cornichons, herbs, mustard, lemon juice, zest, vinegar and curry powder. Mix well to combine. Season the gribiche well with sea salt flakes and freshly ground black pepper.

Toss the cooled asparagus with the gribiche and olive oil, then spoon it liberally on top of the buttered toast. Top with chervil and drizzle with extra olive oil.

Angry Eggs 'n' Greasy Bouncers

1 teaspoon sea salt flakes
¼ teaspoon garlic powder
¼ teaspoon cayenne pepper
4 slices white bread
30 g (1 oz) cheddar, grated or
    cut into four slices
3 tablespoons butter, melted
4 x 6-minute eggs

Combine the salt, garlic powder and cayenne in a small bowl. Set aside.

Top two slices of bread with half the cheese each. Top with the remaining bread slices and brush the tops with half the butter.

Heat a large non-stick frying pan over medium heat and add the sandwiches. Fry for 2 minutes, until golden underneath. Brush the tops with the remaining melted butter. Flip the sandwiches and fry the other sides for 2 minutes, until golden.

Remove the crusts from two sides of each sandwich and then divide into three fat soldiers.

Crack the tops off the eggs and sprinkle them with the spicy salt mix.

Eat immediately.

Here's the thing. I am always quite happy to skip dessert when dining out. I am savoury, salty, saucy, spicy, tangy, umami and hot by nature.

I'll share a crème brûlée or have a bite of gelato, but it's more a full stop than a 'course' for me.

However, when my publisher (who gleefully hosts an annual bake-off at the office) asked for more sweets, I strode towards the challenge with the confidence of a fully made-up drag queen. It was subtle, but the tinge of 'dare' within the request was irresistible.

Most of these recipes have childhood memories attached to them because that's the period in which I fancied sugar the most.

So, I present you with an extra day of sugar and spice and all things nice.

Hope you enjoy it.

Sweet Anytime Treats

Lemon Poppyseed Meringue Cake

This is the serious end
of the book, OK.

3 cups (450 g) plain
  (all-purpose) flour
1 teaspoon baking powder
½ teaspoon bicarbonate
  (baking) soda
½ teaspoon fine salt
2 tablespoons poppyseeds
1 cup (250 ml) buttermilk,
  at room temperature
2 tablespoons finely grated
  lemon zest
2 tablespoons lemon juice

1 cup (250 g) cold salted
  butter, cubed
2 cups (440 g) caster
  (superfine) sugar
1 teaspoon vanilla bean paste
3 eggs, at room temperature

MERINGUE TOP
3 egg whites, at room
  temperature
⅔ cup (150 g) caster
  (superfine) sugar
1 teaspoon cream of tartar

FILLING
1 cup (230 g) cream cheese,
  at room temperature
1 cup (120 g) icing
  (confectioners') sugar,
  plus extra for dusting
1 tablespoon single (pure) cream
½ cup (125 ml) lemon curd

OPTIONAL INGREDIENTS
fear

Poppyseeds are one of the most irritating things to clean up when spilled – it's like they're mildly magnetised and dart around for no apparent reason. Keep a steady hand for this.

Preheat the oven to 160°C (315°F) fan-forced. Grease and line two 22 cm (8½ inch) springform cake tins with baking paper.

In a large bowl, whisk together the flour, baking powder, bicarb, salt and poppyseeds until well mixed. Set aside. Combine the buttermilk, lemon zest and juice in a separate bowl and set aside.

In a standmixer fitted with the paddle attachment, cream the butter, sugar and vanilla on low for 8 minutes, until pale and creamy. The cold cubed butter gives the sugar longer to dissolve as it is beaten, leaving the texture of the creamed butter quite smooth.

Add the eggs, one at a time, beating well after each addition.

With the speed on low, add a quarter of the flour mixture, then a third of the buttermilk mixture. Repeat this process, mixing well after each addition, finishing with the flour.

Pour half of the batter into each of the tins. Place ONE cake into the oven and cook for 40 minutes (set the other tin of batter aside for now). Test for doneness – a skewer poked into the cake should come out clean. Allow this base cake to cool completely in the tin before turning out.*

Meanwhile, make the meringue top. Wash the bowl of the standmixer, then wipe with paper towel soaked in vinegar to remove any residual fat (which will sabotage the meringue).

Use the whisk attachment to whisk the egg whites on high until white and foamy, around 5 minutes. Lower the speed to medium–high and, with the motor running, add 1 tablespoon of sugar at a time until it is all used up and the whites are stiff and glossy, around 7 minutes. Add the cream of tartar and whisk until just combined.

Top the reserved tin of batter with swirls of meringue and bake for 1 hour. Check at 30 minutes, and loosely cover with foil if the peaks are beginning to brown too much. Test for doneness, then remove and set aside to cool.

Beat the cream cheese, icing sugar and cream until smooth, around 5 minutes on high. Set aside a quarter of this icing and a quarter of the lemon curd for the topping.

Place the cooled base cake on a plate and evenly spread the remaining icing and lemon curd over. Carefully place the meringue-crowned cake on top. Artfully dollop on the reserved icing and curd, and dust with icing sugar.

* If you like, level the base cake by trimming off the domed top to create an even flat surface for layering with filling.

Serves 10–12

Sticky Date Brioche

To consume, wear woolly socks and have a crackling fire in the vicinity.

½ cup (125 ml) whisky

12 medjool dates, seeds removed and finely chopped

3 teaspoons instant yeast

4 cups (600 g) plain (all-purpose) flour, plus extra for dusting the cake tin

1 cup (250 ml) lukewarm milk

⅓ cup (90 g) softened salted butter, cubed

½ cup (110 g) firmly packed soft brown sugar

1 teaspoon fine salt

4 egg yolks

2 tablespoons (30 g) melted salted butter, plus extra for greasing the cake tin

1 egg, whisked, for glazing

BUTTERSCOTCH SAUCE

⅓ cup (90 g) salted butter

1½ cups (330 g) firmly packed soft brown sugar

1 cup (250 ml) single (pouring) cream

OPTIONAL INGREDIENTS

ice cream

This is the ultimate weekend away dessert for a dozen (16 actually). It has après ski vibes, or in my case, avant, durant AND après.

You could halve this recipe if you weren't needing AS much but let me warn you – it reheats embarrassingly well and is a viable breakfast.

Heat the whisky and the dates in a small saucepan with the lid on over medium heat until steaming, then set aside to cool.

In the bowl of a standmixer fitted with the dough hook combine the yeast and flour. With the mixer on low, slowly pour in the lukewarm milk until it's all combined. Next, add the softened butter a little at a time until incorporated into the dough. Add the sugar, salt, whisky and dates, then the egg yolks, one at a time, mixing well after each addition. Continue to mix on low until the texture is smooth and stretchy, around 8 minutes.

Cover the dough with plastic wrap and leave to rise for 2 hours in a warm place; it should double in size.

Grease a 24 x 38 cm (9½ x 15 inch) oval cake tin, 4 cm (1½ inches) deep, with butter and dust with some flour, tapping out any excess.

Knead the dough again for a few minutes then divide it into 16 portions. Roll each portion into a ball and place in the cake tin. Brush each ball generously with melted butter.

Cover with plastic wrap and let the dough rise again for 30 minutes.

Preheat the oven to 180°C (350°F) fan-forced.

After the dough has risen again, press your fingertips into it to create cavities and allow the melted butter to sink in.

Brush the balls of dough with the whisked egg and bake for 30–40 minutes, or until the brioche is golden brown.

When the brioche is almost cooked, make the butterscotch sauce. Place the butter and sugar in a medium saucepan over high heat and stir until melted and paste-like. Gradually add the cream, stirring to combine.

Bring to the boil and cook for 6–8 minutes, or until thickened slightly.

While the brioche is still hot, cut it into 16 pieces in the tin.

Slowly pour half the hot butterscotch sauce over the brioche, letting it soak into the cuts.

Place the remaining sauce in a jug to serve alongside the brioche. Ice cream encouraged.

Serves 16

⅓ cup (90 g) cold salted
    butter, cubed
¾ cup (165 g) firmly packed
    soft brown sugar
2 tablespoons lime juice, plus
    1 tablespoon finely grated zest
1 tablespoon white miso
1 kg pineapple, sliced into circles
    5 mm (¼ inch) thick, then peeled
    and cored*
½ cup (60 g) toasted macadamias,
    coarsely chopped

2 square sheets ready-made
    frozen puff pastry
½ cup (130 g) coconut yoghurt

OPTIONAL INGREDIENTS
tinned pineapple – you could
certainly give this recipe a whack
with tinned instead of fresh

The pine-lime flavour combo always reminds me of my dad and holidays on the Central Coast of NSW as a kid. Between sunburns, he'd blare Tone Loc and swerve the car up and down the empty cul de sac, us kids squealing in delight while rolling around in the back seat.

It was the 80s. Life was punky, cool and fun (and possibly rather damaging, but that's a conversation for a therapist). Pine lime Splice ice creams were the sweet treats we licked between bouts of misadventure.

Bringing us skidding into the 2020s is the addition of miso, and I, for one, am glad we made it.

In a large (25 cm/10 inch) non-stick ovenproof frying pan over medium heat, melt the butter, sugar, lime juice and miso and bring to a simmer. Add the pineapple in batches and simmer, turning once, until tender (this

should take 2–3 minutes in total). Set the slices aside on a tray lined with baking paper and allow to cool. Reserve the syrup.

Preheat the oven to 200°C (400°F) fan-forced.

Place half of the macadamia nuts in the same ovenproof frying pan, then top with the pineapple rings, overlapping. Pour half the reserved syrup on top, then cover the fruit with both sheets of puff pastry, tucking it in at the sides. Bake until puffed and golden, around 25 minutes.

Use oven mitts or some handy tea towels to flip the hot frying pan onto a serving plate (this can be deftly done by lining up the pan and the plate, grabbing and flipping). Beware: you are playing with hot toffee.

Top with the remaining macadamia nuts and the lime zest. Serve warm with the extra syrup and coconut yoghurt.

* Usually one would peel, slice, then core a pineapple. However, because of this brilliant cookie-cutter hack, it's slice first, then peel and core – resulting in machine-perfect rings. It means you need to locate a set of round cutters – although rustically sliced pineapple would be lovely too.

Serves 6–8

Miso Pine Lime
Tarte Tatin

Careening down memory
lane with this one.

Mum's Rockmelon Ice

It's the food version of having
diamonds on the soles of your shoes.

750 g (1 lb 10 oz) rockmelon
  (canteloupe), peeled, deseeded
  and roughly chopped
1 cup (220 g) caster
  (superfine) sugar
1¼ cups (310 ml) fresh pink
  grapefruit juice
1 punnet (125 g) raspberries,
  frozen*

OPTIONAL INGREDIENTS
prosecco

This one is a reincarnation of my mum's favourite icy delight. Fresh and spritely, it is perfect as is but equally delicious on ice cream or plopped into a glass with some vodka and prosecco for a summer spritz.

Start off by blitzing the rockmelon in a food processor, then strain the purée through a sieve. You should end up with 2 cups (500 ml) of juice.

Dissolve the sugar in the grapefruit juice in a medium saucepan over medium-high heat for 4 minutes. Simmer for 3 minutes to thicken the syrup slightly, then cover and set aside to cool.

Add the rockmelon juice to the cooled syrup and stir to combine.

Pour the mixture into a 20 x 32 cm (8 x 12½ inch) cake tin, 3 cm (1¼ inches) deep.

Cover with foil and place in the freezer overnight.

Use a fork to roughly break and mush up the frozen mixture.

Serve with frozen raspberries.

* Use a punnet of fresh raspberries that you have frozen, not the store-bought frozen ones that get mauled and mushed in the packaging process. Freezing your own fresh berries means they are glistening jubes of perfection. And you'll be able to try them before freezing to make sure they are super sweet.

Serves 16 as a little ice cup

Berry-Mallow Shortcake

Shortcake. Literally a
cake that is short.

CAKE BATTER

1 cup (90 g) desiccated coconut, plus a little extra for sprinkling
1 cup (220 g) caster (superfine) sugar
1 cup (250 ml) tinned coconut milk
1 cup (150 g) self-raising flour, sifted

STRAWBERRY TOPPING

9 x strawberries, halved lengthways
7 x pink marshmallows, halved
1 tablespoon strawberry jam, plus more for serving

OPTIONAL INGREDIENTS

marshmallows

I am in neither NWA nor that harder, tougher crowd, CWA, but making this cake makes me feel a bit puffy about myself.

Not only does the 1:1:1:1 mix situation calm me down, but the outcome is pretty spesh.

Now, hold onto your pretty pants, it is/was vegan ... until the marshmallows. But, quite frankly, you could make it without these and I would still love it.

The texture is fluffy, sweet and chewy, like a giant coconut macaroon – not to be confused with a macaron.

Preheat the oven to 180°C (350°F) fan-forced.

Grease a 22 cm (8½ inch) round cake tin, 7 cm (2¾ inches) deep, and line it with baking paper. I used this super cute heart-shaped tin, which is 21 x 22 cm (8 x 8½ inches), give or take.

In a large bowl, mix the batter ingredients together well. Pour the batter into the tin and spread to the edges.

Place the strawberries cut-side up in a line across the middle of the cake.

Place in the oven and bake for 30 minutes. Remove the cake and place the cut marshmallows on either side of the strawberries. Bake for a further 10 minutes (or just continue cooking if you aren't including the marshies!).

Allow the cake to cool in the tray until the marshmallows have set, around 10 minutes. Turn the cake out onto a large flat plate and then quickly flip it back over onto a wire rack lined with baking paper so that it's the right way up.

Microwave the jam for 30 seconds and then brush the runny jam over the strawberries.

Dust with some more desiccated coconut and serve with additional warmed runny strawberry jam.

Serves 6–8

BEETROOT JAM
1 large beetroot, leaves trimmed
and skin on
¼ cup (55 g) caster
(superfine) sugar

FILLING
1 cup (230 g) cream cheese
½ cup (60 g) icing
(confectioners') sugar

PIES
½ cup (125 g) cold unsalted
butter, coarsely chopped
1 cup (220 g) firmly packed soft
brown sugar

1 large cold egg
1½ cups (220 g) plain
(all-purpose) flour
½ cup (40 g) unsweetened
cocoa powder, sifted
½ teaspoon bicarbonate
(baking) soda
pinch of fine salt
1½ cups (225 g) dark chocolate,
chopped, and/or choc chips, or
a mix of dark and milk chocolate

OPTIONAL INGREDIENTS
a dislike for beetroot

I have this urge to hide loathed ingredients in recipes and feed them to my family, who in turn LOVE it. It really fills my cup, you know, winning that kind of war.

So many of us have grown up being forced to eat things we don't like and threatened with blindness and our arms falling off if we don't. This way I feel like we all win.

The target was my husband and his beet disgust. He ate this with glee.

And while I personally don't think this is the BEST way to enjoy the earthy sweetness of the beautiful betanin-filled root, it does prove a point: everyone/thing can be delicious with the right wingman.

To make the beetroot jam, steam the beetroot for 20–30 minutes until tender. It should be easily pierced with a sharp knife when done. Allow it to cool, then peel and blitz in a food processor.

In a small saucepan over medium-high heat, bring ½ cup (125 ml) of the beetroot purée and the caster sugar to the boil, stirring. Reduce the heat to low and simmer for

2–3 minutes, until reduced by half. Remove from the heat and allow to cool. This makes ¼ cup (60 ml) of beetroot jam. Set aside.*

For the filling, in the bowl of a standmixer fitted with the paddle attachment, beat the cream cheese and icing sugar on medium-high for 3 minutes, until smooth. Place this into a piping bag and into the fridge ready to go.

Now the pies. In the standmixer again, cream the butter and sugar on low for 8 minutes, until pale and creamy. Add the egg and beat until just combined. Add the flour, cocoa, bicarb soda, salt and half of the beetroot jam. Beat on low speed until a soft cookie dough forms, around 5 minutes.

Add the chunks of chocolate and stir well. I did this by hand so the beater didn't break up the chunks too much.

Divide the dough into six pieces, roughly 150 g (5½ oz) each. Divide each piece into two pieces: ⅔ for the base, ⅓ for the top.

Use your fingers to mould each base into an 11 cm (4¼ inch)

patty. Create a slight indent in the base with a 1 cm (½ inch) rim to hold the cream cheese and jam, then mould each top piece into a slightly smaller, 9.5 cm (3½ inch), lid.

Pipe 1 tablespoon of the cream cheese mixture onto the centre of the bases, then dollop 1 teaspoon of beetroot jam on top. Place the lids on the whoopie pies and squish the sides of the bases up to join together with the lids to completely enclose the cream cheese and jam. You may need to sculpt them a bit to shape them back into cookies.

Place them on a baking tray lined with baking paper and freeze for 20 minutes.

Meanwhile, preheat the oven to 180°C (350°F) fan-forced.

Bake for 20 minutes. Rest for 10 minutes on a wire rack. Break open. Eat. Burn mouth.

---

* Leftovers can be stored in an airtight container in the fridge for 1 week.

Makes 6 whopping whoopie pies!

Beet Whoopie Pies

I go below the belt when trying to get an ingredient across the line by pairing it with chocolate.

Yogalatte

Best eaten wearing
(in)activewear.

¼ cup (60 ml) espresso coffee
1 cup (125 g) icing
   (confectioners') sugar
2 cups (520 g) Greek-style yoghurt

OPTIONAL INGREDIENTS
summer – don't wait for warmth
to make this!

Halfway between ranting about not having time to do yoga or go to Pilates my mind merged the two words into the perfect portmanteau – and the yogalatte recipe was born.

It's tangy, sweet and caffeinated. It feels mature enough to have after dinner but fun enough to have during the day.

I actually don't care when you have it, it has three ingredients and is as easy AF (which is the most important thing for me – possibly before flavour when it comes to sweets).

Combine the warm espresso and icing sugar in a vessel and mix well. If the espresso is cold, then warm it slightly so everything melts together. Set aside to cool.

Add this mixture to the yoghurt and mix well.

Freeze completely in ice cube trays for a minimum of 4 hours.

Once frozen, process in the food processor until smooth.

Serve immediately.

You could churn this in an ice-cream machine instead, or freeze it like granita to fork-shave.

Serves 6

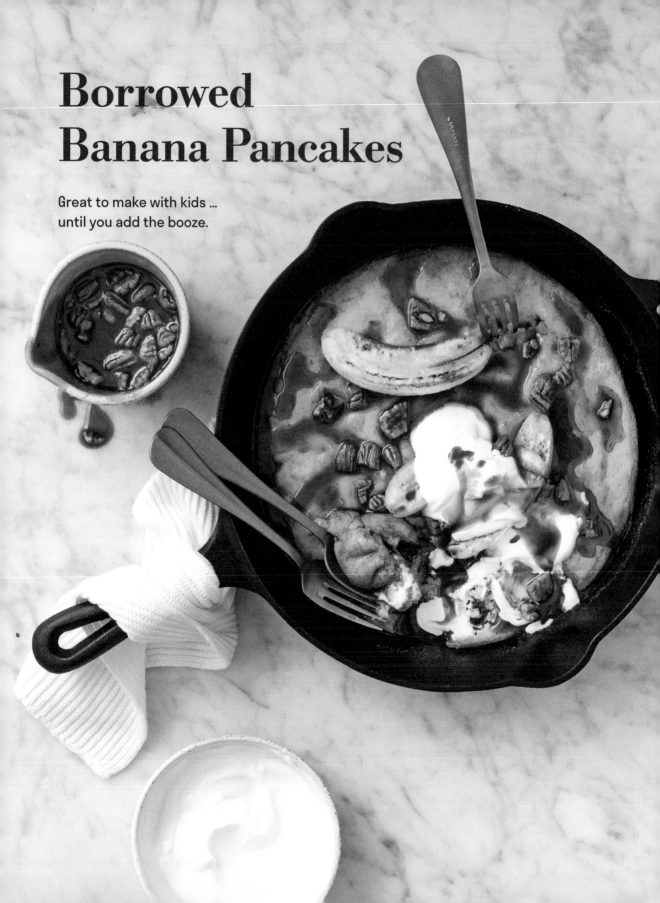

Borrowed Banana Pancakes

Great to make with kids ...
until you add the booze.

2 overripe bananas, mashed,
  plus 2 small bananas, halved
  lengthways
1 egg
¼ cup (35 g) plain
  (all-purpose) flour
½ cup (70 g) self-raising flour
1 cup (250 ml) milk
50 g (1¾ oz) salted butter

CARAMEL SAUCE
1 cup (220 g) firmly packed
  soft brown sugar
⅓ cup (80 ml) whisky
¼ cup (60 ml) golden syrup
50 g (1¾ oz) salted butter

OPTIONAL INGREDIENTS
toasted pecans and
Greek-style yoghurt

My friend Usher does two things really well: wine, and delicious morning-after banana pancakes. He's given me the recipe for both, but I can't be bothered with the wine; the pancakes seem far easier.

And true to form, I have jumped from a stack of pancakes to one big flat pancake, which makes sense for sharing with a cutie. There's no waiting between pancake flipping.

I've also made a luxuriously boozy caramel to pour all over it, which I have been warned is an excessive and wasteful use of Usher's rare batch whisky. So feel free to sub this out for your preferred golden liquor.

Preheat the oven to 200°C (400°F) fan-forced.

Combine the mashed banana, egg, flours and milk in a medium bowl and mix well.

Heat half the butter in a large ovenproof frying pan over medium–low heat.

Once the butter is bubbling, pour all of the batter into the centre of the pan and fry until bubbles form on top. Transfer the pan to the oven for 15 minutes to cook through. It will be golden and sponge-like when done.

Meanwhile, for the caramel sauce, stir the brown sugar, whisky, golden syrup and butter in a small saucepan over medium heat until the sugar has dissolved. Simmer for 2 minutes, then take off the heat and keep warm.

Finally, heat the remaining 25 g (1 oz) of butter in a frying pan over medium heat, add the halved bananas and cook for 2–3 minutes on each side, until golden.

Top the hot pancake with the fried bananas and the warm caramel sauce and serve straight from the frying pan.

Serves 2

375 g (13 oz) blueberries,
   fresh or frozen
375 g (13 oz) blackberries,
   fresh or frozen
½ cup (125 ml) berry jam
juice and finely grated zest
   of 1 orange
1½ cups (330 g) caster
   (superfine) sugar
1 teaspoon cinnamon
5 sheets ready-made frozen
   shortcrust pastry

1 kg (2 lb 4 oz) fresh ricotta
1 teaspoon vanilla bean paste
1 egg, plus an extra egg,
   whisked together with
   1 tablespoon milk, for glazing
2 teaspoons lemon thyme
1 tablespoon raw sugar

OPTIONAL INGREDIENTS
cream to serve

A perfect summer pie with completely interchangeable fruit. Do peach, strawberry, whatever you like, just don't omit the lemon thyme because it makes this dessert really sophisticated – and not even in a smarmy way.

Place the berries, jam and orange juice in a bowl to macerate for 20 minutes.

Meanwhile, combine ½ cup (110 g) of the caster sugar and the cinnamon in a small bowl.

Lay the pastry sheets out on your benchtop and sprinkle the cinnamon sugar on top. Carefully fold the corners of each sheet into the middle (see the little photo)*. Stack the folded sheets on top of each other and pat them down to push out any air. Roll the pastry out into a rustic 40 cm (16 inch) circle, around 5 mm (¼ inch) thick.

Place the pastry on a baking tray lined with baking paper and pop in the fridge for 20 minutes.

Preheat the oven to 200°C (400°F) fan-forced.

Combine the ricotta, vanilla, one egg, orange zest, remaining 1 cup (220 g) caster sugar and the lemon thyme in a large bowl and mix well. Set aside.

Strain the macerated berries over a bowl, reserving both the liquid and the fruit.

Once the pastry has had time to rest and chill, remove it from the fridge and spread the ricotta mixture in the centre, leaving a 5 cm (2 inch) clean edge. The ricotta layer will be around 3 cm (1¼ inches) thick.

Place the drained fruit on top and fold the edges up around the ricotta.

Brush the pastry with egg wash and sprinkle with raw sugar.

Bake for 15 minutes, until golden brown and bubbling.

Allow to cool before cutting.

Serve with a drizzle of the reserved macerating juice.

* Pimping store-bought pastry is a situation I can't get enough of.

Serves 8

Any Berry
Lemon
Thyme Tart

A pretty fabulous showstopper.

Hippyish Pie

Simple pleasures is an
understatement. This recipe
gives you access to full-
blown organic endorphins.

1 tablespoon milk, for glazing
½ teaspoon demerara sugar,
    for sprinkling

FILLING
1 kg (2 lb 4 oz) pumpkin,
    peeled and seeds removed,
    chopped into chunks
350 g (12 oz) carrots,
    chopped into chunks
⅓ cup (65 g) raw sugar
¼ cup (60 ml) lemon juice

1 tablespoon finely
    grated lemon zest
1 teaspoon golden syrup
1 tablespoon sultanas
½ teaspoon nutmeg
1 teaspoon mixed spice
½ teaspoon cinnamon

PIE PASTRY
1 cup (150 g) wholemeal
    (whole-wheat) plain flour
1 cup (150 g) self-raising flour

pinch of sea salt flakes
⅔ cup (160 g) cold salted
    butter, cubed
1 egg
2 tablespoons caster
    (superfine) sugar
1 teaspoon cinnamon

OPTIONAL INGREDIENTS
nakedness and warmed cream

The C on the top of this pie stands for Charlotte, my sister, who helped me work out the mystery of the spices in the pie. As kids, we would sit naked in a galvanised bath in front of the kitchen campfire, warm from flames on one side and chilly from the evening air on the other. We'd eat bowls of this warm pie with cream – it's one of my favourite memories.

Do yourself a favour, make this, run a bath and eat it there.

I've made this with wholemeal flour because that's what Mum did – it kind of felt like punishment as a kid, but now I get it. All consumption, like good deeds, works on a checks and balances system, and I owe my body a lot of wholemeal flour.

Preheat the oven to 200°C (400°F) fan-forced.

Steam the pumpkin and carrots for 15 minutes, or until tender.

Blend the pumpkin, carrots, sugar, lemon juice and zest in a food processor until smooth. Stir through the golden syrup, sultanas and spices and set aside.

For the pastry, blend all the ingredients in a food processor until the mixture resembles breadcrumbs. Then knead it together on a lightly floured surface to form a pastry dough.

Cut off a quarter of the pastry and set aside.

Roll out three-quarters of the pastry into a circle until it's 5 mm thick, then press into a greased 24 cm (9½ inch) shallow old-school pie tin. You could use a quiche tin if you can't find one like this.

Fill the case with the pumpkin mixture and level it out. Brush the edges with milk.

Roll out the remaining quarter of the pastry and place it on top of the pie. Use the back of a spoon to cut/press the edges to seal. Decorate the pie with the leftover scraps of dough – letters, leaves, roses, whatever you like. When I was a kid this was one of the bits we loved the most – and picking them off to eat them once cooked.

Brush the pie lid all over with more milk and sprinkle with the demerara sugar.

Bake for approximately 1 hour, or until golden.

Allow to cool down to warm before serving. It is crumbly and comforting – embrace it, we've all been like that.

Serves 6

Snack, Crackle & Chew

Three ice-cream toppings – each superb on its own, but when
combined you have an instant Snickers-style sundae.

Makes toppings for 4

Pantry Crumble

½ cup (70 g) plain
   (all-purpose) flour
¼ cup (60 g) firmly packed
   soft brown sugar
⅓ cup (50 g) nuts and/or seeds*
1 teaspoon finely grated
   lemon zest
¼ cup (60 g) cold salted butter,
   cubed
½ cup (15 g) rice bubbles

Preheat the oven to 180°C (350°F)
fan-forced and line a baking tray
with baking paper.

In a bowl, combine the flour, sugar,
mixed nuts and seeds and lemon
zest. Add the chopped butter and
combine using your fingertips
until it resembles breadcrumbs.
Stir through the rice bubbles.

Spread out on the baking tray
and bake for 10 minutes.

* For this crumble you can use whatever
nuts/seeds/muesli scraps you can find
in the pantry – it's about the sugar and
butter, really.

Choc-top

1 cup (150 g) dark
   chocolate, chopped
¼ cup (60 ml) coconut oil

First, chuck out that weird
chemical topping that you
bought from the store.

Combine the chocolate and
coconut oil in a glass bowl and
microwave for 30 seconds.
Stir well and microwave for
another 30 seconds.

Peanut Schmeer

¾ cup (215 g) crunchy
   peanut butter
½ cup (125 ml) maple syrup
2 tablespoons hot water

Combine all ingredients together.
That's it. This is good on rice
crackers too. Anywhere really.

Condiments

This section is just a lecture really. Don't waste anything. Pickle it, blend it or rub it with spice. But it's also a hack page. A few quick notes to remind you that we all get to have a second wind, so hit the ground running when you do.

Basic Pickle

½ cup (125 ml) white vinegar
2 teaspoons caster sugar
1 teaspoon sea salt flakes

ADDITIONS
½–1 teaspoon each star anise,
coriander root, mustard seeds,
dill, fennel seeds, cumin, etc.

Combine the vinegar, sugar and
salt with 1 cup (250 ml) water,
then plonk anything into it: ginger,
cucumber, carrot, onion – it works
for everything. Spice it up with
some of the suggested additions.

Curry Pickle

500 g (1 lb 2 oz) vegetables
of your choice, trimmed
if necessary
¼ cup (125 ml) fine sea salt
1 cup (250 ml) white vinegar
½ cup (110 g) caster sugar
1 dried bay leaf
1 teaspoon mustard seeds
1 tablespoon curry powder
1 teaspoon turmeric powder
1 dried red chilli

Toss the trimmed veg in the salt
and set aside.

Simmer the rest of the ingredients
and 1 cup (250 ml) water on the
stovetop just until the sugar
dissolves.

Rinse the salt from the veg and
place the veg in a sealable jar.

Pour the pickle juice over the veg
while still warm, seal and place in
the fridge overnight. Store in the
fridge for up to 1 week.

Baby Beshy

25 g (1 oz) salted butter
1½ tablespoons flour
¼ cup (60 ml) milk

Melt the butter, then add the flour
and stir to form a golden paste.
Whisk in the milk, then stir over low
heat until it thickens. Season well.
You can add more milk/liquid if you
need. Add ½ cup (50 g) cheese of
your choice to make a beautifully
creamy cheese sauce.

This recipe can be doubled
or quadrupled (I seem to use
it often!).

Chilli Crisp

¼ cup (20 g) chilli flakes
2 tablespoons sesame seeds
1 teaspoon fine salt
1 teaspoon chicken-style
   stock powder
2 garlic cloves, crushed
1 cup (250 ml) peanut oil
1 tablespoon crispy fried shallots
1 teaspoon szechuan
   peppercorns

Combine the chilli flakes, sesame
seeds, salt, stock powder and
garlic in a heatproof bowl and
set aside.

Heat the peanut oil, fried shallots
and peppercorns in a medium
saucepan over medium–low
heat until the mixture simmers.
Continue cooking for 2–3 minutes,
then carefully pour it over the
spice mix, allowing it to crackle.
Let it cool, then store in a jar in the
fridge for up to 3 weeks.

L > R
Cucumber & Dill in Basic Pickle
Pickle Curry Cauli Pickle
Young Ginger in Basic Pickle
Baby Beshy
Chilli Crisp

Scrap Pesto

25 g (1 oz) leafy stuff (carrot tops, spinach, rocket, kale)

25 g (1 oz) soft herbs (basil, parsley, mint, coriander)

5 g (⅛ oz) woody herbs (thyme, rosemary, oregano)

2 tablespoons nuts (almonds, pine nuts, walnuts, hazelnuts, macadamias)

25 g (1 oz) hard cheese (parmy, pecorino, goat)

1 small garlic clove, crushed

2 teaspoons something acidic (lemon juice, red wine vinegar)

⅓–½ cup (80–125 ml) extra virgin olive oil, depending on how loose you like pesto

Blend the ingredients in a food processor until smooth, chunky or loose – however you like it. Store in an airtight container in the fridge for up to 3 days.

Use on pasta, toast, eggs, whatevs.

Bready Pesto

½ cup something chunky (sun-dried toms, olives, artichokes, deli veg, roast veg)

1 garlic clove

½ cup (50 g) hard cheese (parmy, pecorino, goat)

2 teaspoons chilli flakes

1 teaspoon mustard

5 g (⅛ oz) woody herbs (thyme, rosemary, oregano)

2 teaspoons something acidic (lemon juice, red wine vinegar)

½ cup (125 g) extra virgin olive oil

1 cup (110 g) breadcrumbs

Blend everything but the breadcrumbs in a food processor until smooth, chunky or loose – however you like it. Stir through the breadcrumbs then store in an airtight container in the fridge for up to 3 days.

It's good as a crust for baked things and great on pasta.

Coconut Sambal

3 tablespoons crispy fried shallots

3 tablespoons desiccated coconut

1 teaspoon chilli flakes

½ teaspoon ground coriander seeds

1 teaspoon makrut lime leaf, crushed

1 teaspoon sea salt flakes

Combine the ingredients and store in an airtight container for up to 3 weeks.

Add some fresh lime zest on the day of serving (it will turn brown if you add it sooner).

Mexican Seasoning

2 tablespoons dried oregano

2 tablespoons chilli flakes

1½ tablespoons ground cumin

1 tablespoon ground coriander seeds

2 teaspoons ground cinnamon

1 tablespoon garlic powder

1 tablespoon onion powder

Combine and store in an airtight container for 3 weeks.

Everything Bagel Seasoning

⅓ cup (55 g) garlic granules

⅓ cup (25 g) dried onion flakes

⅔ cup (100 g) white sesame seeds

⅓ cup (50 g) black sesame seeds

¼ cup (30 g) fennel seeds

¼ cup (40 g) poppy seeds

Combine and store in an airtight container for up to 3 weeks.

L > R

Scrap Pesto
Bready Pesto made with sun-dried tomato
Coconut Sambal
Mexican Seasoning
Everything Bagel Seasoning

Thank You

I feel incredibly fortunate to have grown up eating produce grown on land that has been cared for for over 50,000 years by the Traditional Owners of Country throughout Australia. Specifically in my life, the Gadigal people of the Darkinjung, Dharug and Eora Nations. I recognise their continuing connection to land, water and culture. Along with paying my respects to their Elders past, present and emerging, I also commit to the continued care of this beautiful land where we all live, work and play.

I'd like to extend my deep appreciation to all First Nations peoples on this planet. Without their traditions of caring for the environment, food culture would be an undeniably dull space.

I am grateful for every new food experience, from the simplest to the most complex. It's these inspirational delights that energise this book from beginning to end.

The Cabin Staff: Jaimee, Katja and Breesa. We cooked and created together, and I could not have achieved this book without them. Aside from their passion for food, the killer quips made every day ridiculously fun.

Flying Co Share: Simon – as always in the studio – who I am sure came for the daily degustation but paid his way in a beautiful gallery of BTS. I am forever grateful.

Ground Crew: aka photographers Ben, William and Simon, who support and help me grow. They share insights, knowledge and time – I am indebted to you all.

The Air Traffic Controllers: my publishing team at Murdoch Books. Jane, who once again guided and encouraged me and, of course, fulfilled my glitter cover dreams. The ever-patient team who played deadline tag with me constantly – Megan, VB, Martine and Madeleine. Thank you, team MB.

The Supply Chain: the shops in my hood that support small and seasonal farming, whose staff love what they do and have become great friends. Plus, the artisans, makers and creators of the beautiful bits and pieces you'll see throughout this book, who are passionate about the continued success of food in print media: Akeramic, Cultiver, Studio Enti, Country Road and Major & Tom.

Inflight Entertainment: as always, the Instagram community, which cajoles, ridicules and champions food, laughter and play. This community inspires me daily. You guys feel like friends.

And, of course, after a strange journey using travel analogies on this page, we reach our Final Destination: Home! It's where the heart beats, aches, imagines, creates, empties and fills … daily.

Andy, James, Beau and Winter. Thank you for trying everything even when you weren't in the mood, laughing with/at me/each other and reinforcing my 'crumb + fry it' theory.

Index

A

Aioli 121
Alfredo 'Shroom Soufra 92–93
apples
  Only Sides (vegetarian roast dinner) 50–51
  Sweet Remy Slaw 146–147
Arancini, Cuban 100–101
artichokes
  artichokes with aioli and garlic butter 120–121
  Calzleme 104–105
  Muffuletta Pie 90–91
  One-Pot Business (pasta with artichokes and olives) 12–13
  Pizza Rice 44–45
  Spinach, Feta, Basil (spinach dip) 135
  stuffed artichokes 120–121
  Summer Mini (green vegetable soup with pesto) 66–67
asparagus
  Asparagus, Parmy, Lemon, Crumb (salad or side) 161
  Asparagus with Curried Gribiche 189
  French Frills (salad of young greens) 152–153
  Spring Goddess Risotto 74–75
aubergines. *See* eggplants
avocados
  Burrito Bowl 154–155
  Chilaquiles 178–179
  Cult Bowl (quinoa bowl with pumpkin, avo and pickles) 168–169
  Fried Mini Tacos 122–123
  Silky Folds Taco (tacos with scrambled eggs, corn and avo) 170–171

B

Baby Beshy (béchamel sauce) 215
Bagel Seasoning, Everything 216
Banana Pancakes, Borrowed 206–207
beans, black. *See* black beans
beans, cannellini. *See* cannellini beans
beans, green. *See* green beans
béchamel sauce (Baby Beshy) 215
beetroot
  Beet, Almond, Horseradish (beetroot dip) 135
  Beet Falafel 96–97
  Beet Whoopie Pies 202–203
  Seriously Glistening Salad, A (roast vegetable and lentil salad with goat's curd) 158–159

black beans
  Burrito Bowl 154–155
  Nachos Mess 48–49
blackberries: Any Berry Lemon Thyme Tart 208–209
blueberries: Any Berry Lemon Thyme Tart 208–209
bok choy
  Crispy Edge (rice and greens with fried eggs and chilli) 176–177
  Ribbons in Crackling Oil 24–25
  Spicy Satay Minute Noodles 82
Bombay Wish Potatoes 40–41
bread. *See also* toast and toasties
  Bready Pesto 216
  Canned Bread Soup 78–79
  Deep-Pan Aperitivo (focaccia with tomato and olives) 116–117
  Eggs Niçoise Breakfast Salad 180–181
  Golden Crouton, The (tomato salad with croutons and burrata) 144–145
  Potato Bread Soup 60–61
  stale bread, how to revive 9
brie: Toffee Cheese & Fancy Crack (toffee brie with crackers) 128–129
Brioche, Sticky Date 194–195
broad beans: Herby Chunk Pesto 35
broccoli and broccolini
  Bombay Wish Potatoes 40–41
  Burnt Broc Mac 'n' Cheese 35
  Crispy Edge (rice and greens with fried eggs and chilli) 176–177
  Ribbons in Crackling Oil 24–25
  Scrap Burgers 94–95
  Summer Mini (green vegetable soup with pesto) 66–67
brussels sprouts: Sticky Maple Mustard Brussels 126–127
Buffalo Jals (stuffed jalapeños) 118–119
burgers: Scrap Burgers 94–95
burrata: Golden Crouton, The (tomato salad with croutons and burrata) 144–145
Burrito Bowl 154–155

C

cabbage
  Kimchi Rice Cakes 88–89
  Noodle Nut Salad 148–149
  Sweet Remy Slaw 146–147
Caesar salad: Nicy Cez (Caesar Niçoise salad) 142–143
cakes
  Beet Whoopie Pies 202–203

Berry-Mallow Shortcake 200–201
  Lemon Poppyseed Meringue Cake 192–193
  Calzleme 104–105
cannellini beans
  Canned Bread Soup 78–79
  White Bean Parmy (white bean dip) 135
canteloupe: Mum's Rockmelon Ice 198–199
capsicums
  Fennel Ragu on Polenta 64–65
  Golden Crouton, The (tomato salad with croutons and burrata) 144–145
  Pizza Rice 44–45
caramel
  Borrowed Banana Pancakes 206–207
  Sticky Date Brioche 194–195
cauliflower
  Cheeseburger Rolls 131
  Honey Soy Cauli 42–43
  Mulligatawny & a Flatty 72–73
  Peri-Peri Popcorn Cauli 102–103
cavolo nero. *See also* kale
  Green Eggs & Jam Tart (cavolo nero tart with onion jam) 182–183
  Summer Mini (green vegetable soup with pesto) 66–67
celeriac
  Sweet Remy Slaw 146–147
  Thick & Delicious (corn chowder) 76–77
Cheese & Tomato Lasagne 26–27
Cheeseburger Rolls 131
chickpeas
  Beet Falafel 96–97
  Quick & Curried (curried chickpea and tomato soup) 68–69
  Scrap Burgers 94–95
Chilaquiles 178–179
Chilli Crisp (chilli oil) 215
Chinese broccoli
  Crispy Edge (rice and greens with fried eggs and chilli) 176–177
  Ribbons in Crackling Oil 24–25
Chinese water spinach: Ribbons in Crackling Oil 24–25
chips: Disco Fries 112–113
chocolate and cocoa
  Beet Whoopie Pies 202–203
  Choc-top (ice-cream topping) 213
Coconut Sambal 216
coffee: Yogalatte (coffee frozen yoghurt) 204–205
Congee, Mushroom & Miso 62–63

coriander: Chutney 41
corn
    Cuban Arancini 100–101
    Fluffy Corn & Tofu Dumplings 108
    Nachos Mess 48–49
    Silky Folds Taco (tacos with scrambled
        eggs, corn and avo) 170–171
    Spicy Satay Minute Noodles 82
    Sweet Corn Pillows (ravioli) 20–21
    Thick & Delicious (corn chowder) 76–77
    Vietnamese Pancakes (Bánh Xèo)
        186–187
courgettes. See zucchini
crackers: Toffee Cheese & Fancy Crack
    (toffee brie with crackers) 128–129
Crispy Personality Potatoes 55
Crouton, The Golden (tomato salad with
    croutons and burrata) 144–145
Cuban Arancini 100–101
cucumbers
    Noodle Nut Salad 148–149
    Salad Bash (smashed cucumber salad
        with edamame and tofu) 140–141
    Tofu Larb 150–151

D

dates: Sticky Date Brioche 194–195
dips
    Beet, Almond, Horseradish 135
    Spinach, Feta, Basil 135
    White Bean Parmy 135
Disco Fries 112–113
dumplings
    Crispy Eggplant Momos 109
    Fluffy Corn & Tofu Dumplings 108
    Steamed Vegetable Dumplings 108

E

edamame
    Cult Bowl (quinoa bowl with pumpkin,
        avo and pickles) 168–169
    Salad Bash (smashed cucumber
        salad with edamame and tofu)
        140–141
eggplants
    Crispy Eggplant Momos 109
    Mapo Eggplant 80–81
    Muffuletta Pie 90–91
    Stacked Eggplant Parm 52–53
    Ultra Ratta Tarte Tatin (eggplant,
        zucchini and tomato tarte tatin)
        38–39
eggs
    Angry Eggs 'n' Greasy Bouncers (eggs
        with cheese toasties) 189
    Asparagus with Curried Gribiche 189
    Chilaquiles 178–179
    Crispy Edge (rice and greens with fried
        eggs and chilli) 176–177
    Cult Bowl (quinoa bowl with pumpkin,
        avo and pickles) 168–169

    Eggs Niçoise Breakfast Salad 180–181
    French Rarebit 172–173
    Grated Hard Egg Salad 188
    Green Eggs & Jam Tart (cavolo nero tart
        with onion jam) 182–183
    Hash & Egg Muffins 184–185
    In Heaven (coddled eggs with leeks
        and spinach) 166–167
    In Hell (shakshuka) 164–165
    Nicy Cez (Caesar Niçoise salad) 142–143
    Silky Folds Taco (tacos with scrambled
        eggs, corn and avo) 170–171
    Spicy Satay Minute Noodles 82
    Tommy Crumble & Mustard Scram
        (tomato crumble with scrambled
        eggs) 174–175
    Vegan Pad Thai 30–31
Everything Bagel Seasoning 216

F

Falafel, Beet 96–97
Fennel Ragu on Polenta 64–65
flatbreads (Flatties) 41, 73
    Calzleme 104–105
    Deep-Pan Aperitivo (focaccia with
        tomato and olives) 116–117
Flatty. See flatbreads (Flatties)
focaccia: Deep-Pan Aperitivo (focaccia
    with tomato and olives) 116–117
French Rarebit 172–173
Fries, Disco 112–113

G

garlic: A Private Artichoke (artichokes with
    aioli and garlic butter) 120–121
gnocchi
    Baked Pumpkin Gnocchi 28–29
    Stacked Eggplant Parm 52–53
    Supergreens Gnudi 14–15
Gnudi, Supergreens 14–15
goat's curd
    Full Metal Jackets (stuffed jacket
        potatoes) 86–87
    Herby Chunk Pesto 35
    Seriously Glistening Salad, A (roast
        vegetable and lentil salad with
        goat's curd) 158–159
Golden Crouton, The (tomato salad with
    croutons and burrata) 144–145
Grate Soup 83
green beans
    Beans, Tomato, Feta (salad or side) 161
    Eggs Niçoise Breakfast Salad 180–181
    French Frills (salad of young greens)
        152–153
    Only Sides (vegetarian roast dinner)
        50–51
Gremolata 65

H

Hash & Egg Muffins 184–185
herbs. See also specific herbs
    Herby Chunk Pesto 35
    how to ice and store 8
    using leftover 8
Hippyish Pie (pumpkin pie) 210–211
Honey Soy Cauli 42–43

I

ice-cream toppings
    Choc-top 213
    Pantry Crumble 213
    Peanut Schmeer 213
ices and other frozen desserts
    Mum's Rockmelon Ice 198–199
    Yogalatte (coffee frozen yoghurt)
        204–205

J

jackfruit: Fried Mini Tacos 122–123
jalapeños: Buffalo Jals (stuffed jalapeños)
    118–119

K

kale. See also cavolo nero
    Canned Bread Soup 78–79
    Cult Bowl (quinoa bowl with pumpkin,
        avo and pickles) 168–169
    Supergreens Gnudi 14–15
Kimchi Rice Cakes 88–89

L

labne: Peach & Panda Salad 156–157
Lady & The Tramp (pasta with pesto, olives
    and capers) 32–33
lasagne: Cheese & Tomato Lasagne 26–27
leeks: In Heaven (coddled eggs with leeks
    and spinach) 166–167
Lemon Poppyseed Meringue Cake
    192–193
lentils
    Mulligatawny & a Flatty 72–73
    Seriously Glistening Salad, A (roast
        vegetable and lentil salad with
        goat's curd) 158–159
lettuce
    Burrito Bowl 154–155
    French Frills (salad of young greens)
        152–153
    how to store 8
    Nicy Cez (Caesar Niçoise salad) 142–143
    Pea Lettuce (pea and lettuce soup with
        cheesy crackers) 58–59
    Tofu Larb 150–151
Loaded Personality Potatoes 55

M

Mac 'n' Cheese, Burnt Broc 35
Mapo Eggplant 80–81
Massaman Skewers 132–133

Mexican Seasoning 216
Mincy Pies 131
miso
    Miso Pine Lime Tarte Tatin 196–197
    Mushroom & Miso Congee 62–63
momos: Crispy Eggplant Momos 109
muffins, English: Hash & Egg Muffins
    184–185
Muffuletta Pie 90–91
Mulligatawny & a Flatty 72–73
mushrooms
    Alfredo 'Shroom Soufra 92–93
    Mincy Pies 131
    Mushroom & Miso Congee 62–63
    90s Scissor Slice (mushroom pizza)
        46–47
    Pizza Rice 44–45
    Steamed Vegetable Dumplings 108
    Vegan Pad Thai 30–31

N
Nachos Mess 48–49
Niçoise salad
    Eggs Niçoise Breakfast Salad 180–181
    Nicy Cez (Caesar Niçoise salad)
        142–143
noodles. See pasta and noodles

O
olives
    Deep-Pan Aperitivo (focaccia with
        tomato and olives) 116–117
    Eggs Niçoise Breakfast Salad 180–181
    Full Metal Jackets (stuffed jacket
        potatoes) 86–87
    Lady & The Tramp (pasta with pesto,
        olives and capers) 32–33
    Nicy Cez (Caesar Niçoise salad) 142–143
    One-Pot Business (pasta with
        artichokes and olives) 12–13
    Pizza Rice 44–45
    Tapenade 116
Only Sides (vegetarian roast dinner)
    50–51
oyster mushrooms: Vegan Pad Thai 30–31

P
Pad Thai, Vegan 30–31
pancakes
    Borrowed Banana Pancakes 206–207
    Kimchi Rice Cakes 88–89
    Vietnamese Pancakes (Bánh Xèo)
        186–187
Pantry Crumble (ice-cream topping) 213
pantry tips 9
papaya: Noodle Nut Salad 148–149
parsley
    Gremolata 65
    Parsley Salad 96–97
parsnips: Only Sides (vegetarian roast
    dinner) 50–51

pasta and noodles
    Angel Hair & Tomato Sunshine 35
    Baked Pumpkin Gnocchi 28–29
    Burnt Broc Mac 'n' Cheese 35
    Golden Pho 83
    Grate Soup 83
    Herby Chunk Pesto 35
    Lady & The Tramp (pasta with pesto,
        olives and capers) 32–33
    Noodle Nut Salad 148–149
    One-Pot Business (pasta with
        artichokes and olives) 12–13
    Ribbons in Crackling Oil 24–25
    Snipped Noodles in Vodka Sauce 22–23
    Spicy Satay Minute Noodles 82
    Stacked Eggplant Parm 52–53
    Supergreens Gnudi 14–15
    Sweet Corn Pillows (ravioli) 20–21
    Vegan Pad Thai 30–31
    Vegemite Cacio e Pepe 16–17
    Zucchini Carbonara 18–19
pastries, pies and tarts
    Alfredo 'Shroom Soufra 92–93
    Any Berry Lemon Thyme Tart 208–209
    Calzleme 104–105
    Cheeseburger Rolls 131
    Green Eggs & Jam Tart (cavolo nero tart
        with onion jam) 182–183
    Hippyish Pie (pumpkin pie) 210–211
    Mincy Pies 131
    Miso Pine Lime Tarte Tatin 196–197
    Muffuletta Pie 90–91
    Ultra Ratta Tarte Tatin (eggplant,
        zucchini and tomato tarte tatin)
        38–39
Peach & Panda Salad (peach and labne
    salad) 156–157
peanuts and peanut butter
    Massaman Skewers 132–133
    Noodle Nut Salad 148–149
    Peanut Schmeer (ice-cream topping)
        213
    Spicy Satay Minute Noodles 82
peas
    French Frills (salad of young greens)
        152–153
    Grated Hard Egg Salad 188
    Herby Chunk Pesto 35
    Only Sides (vegetarian roast dinner)
        50–51
    Pea Lettuce (pea and lettuce soup with
        cheesy crackers) 58–59
    Pesto 67
    Spring Goddess Risotto 74–75
peppers. See capsicums
Peri-Peri Popcorn Cauli 102–103
pesto 67
    Bready Pesto 216
    Herby Chunk Pesto 35
    Scrap Pesto 216
Pho, Golden 83

pickles
    Basic Pickle 215
    Curry Pickle 215
pies. See pastries, pies and tarts
pineapple: Miso Pine Lime Tarte Tatin
    196–197
pizza: 90s Scissor Slice (mushroom pizza)
    46–47
Pizza Rice 44–45
Polenta, Fennel Ragu on 64–65
potatoes
    Bombay Wish Potatoes 40–41
    Cheeseburger Rolls 131
    Crispy Personality Potatoes 55
    Disco Fries 112–113
    Eggs Niçoise Breakfast Salad 180–181
    Full Metal Jackets (stuffed jacket
        potatoes) 86–87
    Giant Stuffed Rosti 98–99
    Grate Soup 83
    Hash & Egg Muffins 184–185
    In Hell (shakshuka) 164–165
    Loaded Personality Potatoes 55
    Only Sides (vegetarian roast dinner)
        50–51
    Potato Bread Soup 60–61
    Potato Brilliance (potato salad) 138–139
    Sorrel Spinach Soup 70–71
    Sticky Personality Potatoes 55
    Thick & Delicious (corn chowder) 76–77
poutine: Disco Fries 112–113
puddings
    Borrowed Banana Pancakes 206–207
    Hippyish Pie (pumpkin pie) 210–211
    Sticky Date Brioche 194–195
pumpkin
    Baked Pumpkin Gnocchi 28–29
    Cult Bowl (quinoa bowl with pumpkin,
        avo and pickles) 168–169
    Hippyish Pie (pumpkin pie) 210–211
    Massaman Skewers 132–133
    Only Sides (vegetarian roast dinner)
        50–51

Q
quinoa: Cult Bowl (quinoa bowl with
    pumpkin, avo and pickles) 168–169

R
Radicchio, Blue Cheese, Walnut, Honey
    (salad or side) 161
rice
    Burrito Bowl 154–155
    Crispy Edge (rice and greens with fried
        eggs and chilli) 176–177
    Cuban Arancini 100–101
    Kimchi Rice Cakes 88–89
    Mushroom & Miso Congee 62–63
    Pizza Rice 44–45
    Spring Goddess Risotto 74–75

ricotta
    Any Berry Lemon Thyme Tart 208–209
    Calzleme 104–105
    Salt & Battery Floral (ricotta-stuffed zucchini flowers) 114–115
    Spinach, Feta, Basil (spinach dip) 135
    Supergreens Gnudi 14–15
    Sweet Corn Pillows (ravioli) 20–21
    Ultra Ratta Tarte Tatin (eggplant, zucchini and tomato tarte tatin) 38–39
Risotto, Spring Goddess 74–75
Rockmelon Ice, Mum's 198–199
Rosti, Giant Stuffed 98–99

S

salads
    Asparagus, Parmy, Lemon, Crumb 161
    Beans, Tomato, Feta 161
    Burrito Bowl 154–155
    Eggs Niçoise Breakfast Salad 180–181
    French Frills (salad of young greens) 152–153
    Golden Crouton, The (tomato salad with croutons and burrata) 144–145
    Grated Hard Egg Salad 188
    Nicy Cez (Caesar Niçoise salad) 142–143
    Noodle Nut Salad 148–149
    Parsley Salad 96
    Peach & Panda Salad (peach and labne salad) 156–157
    Potato Brilliance (potato salad) 138–139
    Radicchio, Blue Cheese, Walnut, Honey 161
    Salad Bash (smashed cucumber salad with edamame and tofu) 140–141
    Seriously Glistening Salad, A (roast vegetable and lentil salad with goat's curd) 158–159
    Sweet Remy Slaw 146–147
Salsa 87
    Salsa Rosso 154
Satay Sauce 133
Scrap Burgers 94–95
Scrap Pesto 216
shakshuka: In Hell 164–165
silverbeet: Crispy Edge (rice and greens with fried eggs and chilli) 176–177
Skewers, Massaman 132–133
Sorrel Spinach Soup 70–71
soufra: Alfredo 'Shroom Soufra 92–93
soups
    Canned Bread Soup 78–79
    Golden Pho 83
    Grate Soup 83
    Mulligatawny & a Flatty 72–73
    Pea Lettuce (pea and lettuce soup with cheesy crackers) 58–59
    Potato Bread Soup 60–61
    Quick & Curried (curried chickpea and tomato soup) 68–69

Sorrel Spinach Soup 70–71
Summer Mini (green vegetable soup with pesto) 66–67
Thick & Delicious (corn chowder) 76–77
spinach
    Calzleme 104–105
    Crispy Edge (rice and greens with fried eggs and chilli) 176–177
    In Heaven (coddled eggs with leeks and spinach) 166–167
    Loaded Personality Potatoes 55
    Muffuletta Pie 90–91
    Sorrel Spinach Soup 70–71
    Spinach, Feta, Basil (spinach dip) 135
    Spring Goddess Risotto 74–75
    Summer Mini (green vegetable soup with pesto) 66–67
    Supergreens Gnudi 14–15
squash. See pumpkin
Sticky Date Brioche 194–195
Sticky Personality Potatoes 55
strawberries: Berry-Mallow Shortcake 200–201
Summer Mini (green vegetable soup with pesto) 66–67
Supergreens Gnudi 14–15
sweet potatoes
    Cheeseburger Rolls 131
    Muffuletta Pie 90–91
    Mulligatawny & a Flatty 72–73

T

tacos
    Fried Mini Tacos 122–123
    Silky Folds Taco (tacos with scrambled eggs, corn and avo) 170–171
Tapenade 116
Tarte Tatin, Ultra Ratta (eggplant, zucchini and tomato tarte tatin) 38–39
tarts. See pastries, pies and tarts
toast and toasties
    Angry Eggs 'n' Greasy Bouncers (eggs with cheese toasties) 189
    Asparagus with Curried Gribiche 189
    French Rarebit 172–173
    Grated Hard Egg Salad 188
    Toffee Cheese & Fancy Crack (toffee brie with crackers) 128–129
tofu
    Fluffy Corn & Tofu Dumplings 108
    Mapo Eggplant 80–81
    S+P Tofu Cups 124–125
    Salad Bash (smashed cucumber salad with edamame and tofu) 140–141
    Tofu Larb 150–151
    Vegan Pad Thai 30–31
tomatoes
    Angel Hair & Tomato Sunshine 35
    Baked Pumpkin Gnocchi 28–29
    Beans, Tomato, Feta (salad or side) 161
    Burrito Bowl 154–155

    Canned Bread Soup 78–79
    Cheese & Tomato Lasagne 26–27
    Deep-Pan Aperitivo (focaccia with tomato and olives) 116–117
    Fennel Ragu on Polenta 64–65
    Golden Crouton, The (tomato salad with croutons and burrata) 144–145
    Grate Soup 83
    In Hell (shakshuka) 164–165
    Nachos Mess 48–49
    Pizza Rice 44–45
    Quick & Curried (curried chickpea and tomato soup) 68–69
    Salsa 87
    Salsa Rosso 154
    Snipped Noodles in Vodka Sauce 22–23
    Stacked Eggplant Parm 52–53
    Tommy Crumble & Mustard Scram (tomato crumble with scrambled eggs) 174–175
    Ultra Ratta Tarte Tatin (eggplant, zucchini and tomato tarte tatin) 38–39

V

Vegemite Cacio e Pepe 16–17
Vietnamese Pancakes (Bánh Xèo) 186–187

W

water spinach: Crispy Edge (rice and greens with fried eggs and chilli) 176–177
White Bean Parmy (white bean dip) 135
wombok
    Kimchi Rice Cakes 88–89
    Noodle Nut Salad 148–149
    Vegan Pad Thai 30–31

Y

yoghurt
    Beet Falafel 96–97
    Yogalatte (coffee frozen yoghurt) 204–205

Z

zucchini
    Grate Soup 83
    Loaded Personality Potatoes 55
    Muffuletta Pie 90–91
    Noodle Nut Salad 148–149
    Spring Goddess Risotto 74–75
    Summer Mini (green vegetable soup with pesto) 66–67
    Ultra Ratta Tarte Tatin (eggplant, zucchini and tomato tarte tatin) 38–39
    Zucchini Carbonara 18–19
zucchini flowers: Salt & Battery Floral (ricotta-stuffed zucchini flowers) 114–115

Published in 2023 by Murdoch Books, an imprint of Allen & Unwin

Murdoch Books Australia
Cammeraygal Country
83 Alexander Street
Crows Nest NSW 2065
Phone: +61 (0)2 8425 0100
murdochbooks.com.au
info@murdochbooks.com.au

Murdoch Books UK
Ormond House
26–27 Boswell Street
London WC1N 3JZ
Phone: +44 (0) 20 8785 5995
murdochbooks.co.uk
info@murdochbooks.co.uk

For corporate orders and custom publishing,
contact our business development team at
salesenquiries@murdochbooks.com.au

Publisher: Jane Morrow
Editorial Manager: Virginia Birch
Design Manager: Megan Pigott
Designer: Madeleine Kane
Editor: Martine Lleonart
Concept, Recipes, Art Direction, Styling and Photography:
Lucy Tweed
Additional Photography: William Meppem and Hannah Blackmore
Home Economists: Jaimee Curdie, Katja Harding-Irmer
and Breesa Swan
Production Director: Lou Playfair

**Murdoch Books acknowledges the Traditional
Owners of the Country on which we live and
work. We pay our respects to all Aboriginal and
Torres Strait Islander Elders, past and present.**

ISBN 978 1 92261 651 7

 A catalogue record for this
book is available from the
National Library of Australia

A catalogue record for this book is available from
the British Library

Colour reproduction by Splitting Image Colour Studio Pty Ltd,
Clayton, Victoria
Printed by Hang Tai Printing Company Limited, China

OVEN GUIDE: You may find cooking times vary depending on
the oven you are using. For fan-forced ovens, as a general
rule, set the oven temperature to 20°C (35°F) lower than
indicated in the recipe.

TABLESPOON MEASURES: We have used 20 ml (4 teaspoon)
tablespoon measures. If you are using a 15 ml (3 teaspoon)
tablespoon add an extra teaspoon of the ingredient for
each tablespoon specified.

10 9 8 7 6 5 4 3 2 1

MIX
Paper | Supporting
responsible forestry
FSC
www.fsc.org
FSC® C023121